Parables for the New Politics

Damhegion y Wleidyddiaeth Newydd

Siôn Rees Williams

Siôn Rees Williams

Copyright © 2015 Siôn Rees Williams

All rights reserved.

ISBN:-10:1512269611
ISBN-13:9781512269611

TO
The lovers of freedom everywhere
ac er cof am f'annwyl dad
John Ellis Williams
20.08.1924 – 07.12.2008.

CONTENTS

Acknowledgments   viii

Introduction   ix

1	The little fishes and the big fish	1
2	The little frogs and the big frogs	9
3	The two men in the pub	17
4	Scottie and Jon Bull	18
5	Jock's birthday party	27
6	The two clouds	31
7	Of nations and shopkeepers	35
8	The four balloons	41
9	The two books	44
10	The house that Jack built	50
11	The three trees	55
12	The caterpillar grows up	58
13	The two suitcases	62

14	The two traffic lights I	66
15	The two traffic lights II	69
16	The boxing match	72
17	*S.S. Anglia*	76
18	Meet the Brittens – A dysfunctional family like no other	85
19	Dear Catriona I …	100
20	Passenger announcement for those travelling by Scot Rail	109
21	Farmer MacDonald	111
22	It's time!	114
23	Tannoy announcement	119
24	The wine connoisseurs	121
25	The sun and the snowflake	124
26	That's charming, darling!	125
27	The chimpanzees	126
28	The two cars	130
29	Angus Alba and his shirts	134
30	How about some wine, Scotland?	142
31	*Gwrthryfel!*	144

32	John	149
33	The bee's knees is the business	157
34	Of mice and ... ?	164
35	An advisory letter to Scottish investors	174
36	Bunny's bid for freedom	182
37	The Scott family trunk	189
38	Mrs Scott's aye test	198
39	The racehorse and the beetle	204
40	Three men in a car	216
41	Mr Scott and his bUNION	224
42	The shark and the turtle	230
43	Angela Alba's having a baby	232
44	Reverend Caledonia and the candles	239
45	Georgia and Andrea	244
46	The flowers in Jon Bull's garden	266
47	The "Freedom Jewel"	273
48	Nobody's-Darling and McDoughnut	278
49	Give us this day ...	289
50	They're all balloons!	295
51	Dear Catriona II ...	301

52	Soup of the Day	305
53	Passenger announcement for those travelling by Free Caledonia Rail	310
54	An eminent psychologist writes …	312
55	Hurricane Nicola	315
56	Carmichael's the Butcher's	322

ACKNOWLEDGMENTS

My thanks to everybody who has read these parables in their original forms, provided me with constructive criticism thereto and encouraged me to continue with them.

Special thanks are due to my wife, Miranda Constance Williams for enduring hours of solitude as I nurtured my creations and for also supplying the (feminine) solution to solving the otherwise intractable (male) problem of disposing of unsuitable items of clothing for the parable of *Angus Alba and his shirts* (Number 29, p. 134). Also, thanks to Karen Bain for supplying the authentic Scots dialogue in *The two men in the pub* (Number 3, p. 17) and in *Angus Alba and his shirts* (Number 29, p. 134). Karen also supplied the basic idea for *How about some wine, Scotland?* (Number 30, p. 142). Additionally, whilst most of these stories have come out of the ether as it were, Hayley Townsend deserves the credit for making me think positively of the connection between monkeys and culture, which gave rise to *The Chimpanzees* (Number 27, p. 126). Charles Docherty wanted me to write a parable in memory of Margo MacDonald and although I at first desisted, a story began to form as I was listening to a candlelit concert in St. Alban's Cathedral. The end result is *Reverend Caledonia and the candles* (Number 44, p. 239). Mags Hart suggested improvements for *It's Time!* (Number 22, p. 114) and Michael McFadyen provided further useful ideas for *Mrs. Scott's aye test* (Number 38, p. 198). I owe a deep debt of gratitude to Christina Shaw and Sabine Asmus for their editing and invaluable, encouraging comments on the totality of the parables. My thanks also to Jim Murison and Paul Colvin for helping with the publishing process.

It goes without saying that any errors, inaccuracies, omissions or things that do not 'work' in the parables are solely my responsibility.

Introduction

A parable, according to the Concise Oxford English Dictionary is "a simple story used to illustrate a moral or spiritual lesson." Now, I don't profess to have any superiority with regard to matters of a moral nor spiritual nature. Rather, these stories are more of a commentary on how I personally perceive Welsh, Scottish, Cornish, Celtic and British history and politics. The first 48 were written prior to the Scottish Independence Referendum of September 2014; numbers 49 to 56 were written after that momentous event. I write in the hope for a brighter future for the nations of Celtia and indeed, obliquely, England.

Yet, whereas I am writing these pieces from an essentially patriotic Welsh and Celtic background – and some may argue, I can do no other – it is pleasing to note that there are others who have read the drafts of these parables elsewhere, are outside Celtia and have enjoyed them. They have even commented that some themes appear to be universal to smaller groups and individuals who are seeking more autonomy and independence for their (usually, but not exclusively minority) languages and cultures from the overbearing presence of a more mighty neighbour. In this regard, Cornishmen share similar experiences to Kosovars, Welshwomen with Catalans and Québecois with the Manx. But there are messages here too for the more powerful neighbours of these people, be they English, French or Spanish or, indeed any others who may (perhaps through no fault of their own) have considered themselves to be top dogs for so long and have neglected, ignored, suppressed or suffocated their own minorities and neighbours.

However, I do not intend to get 'preachy.' The parables all stand alone and can be read in any order and as often (or not!) as is desired by readers. Let the parables speak for themselves, with the hope you will enjoy them as much as I enjoyed composing them.

Dunstable, England
Spring 2015

1 The little fishes and the big fish

Once upon a time, there was a little fish that lived in a river. The little fish was very happy. He could swim where he wanted. He could do what he wanted. He had his own friends, usually the other little fishes. The little fish lived a very happy life. He didn't worry about anything.

Then, one day, a much bigger fish came to the little fish's river.

"I'm going to eat you up," said the big fish.

"Oh no! Please don't do that!" said the little fish.

"Hmmm." The big fish thought for a moment. "OK then," said the big fish, "but from now on, you will do everything I say."

"Errrm, y-y-yes, all right," stuttered the little fish. "Only, please don't eat me."

"Right," said the big fish. "This is what you will do. You will recognise that from henceforth this is *my* river. From now on, what I say goes, both in and on this stretch of water. You will have no rights in the matter. Got that?"

The little fish gasped. But he knew that he would be eaten if he did not agree.

So he said, very softly, "Yes, sir."

"Good," said the big fish. "Now, this is the deal. While I am swimming in *my* river, I want you to eat the little parasites that infect my scales. I must look my best in *my* new domain, you see. This will also provide you with your food, you understand?"

The little fish nodded sadly.

"What is more," the big fish went on, "when there is

any danger about, I will gladly open my mouth for you. You can then swim inside and I will protect you inside my tummy until the danger is past."

"B-b-b-ut" stammered the little fish, "t-t-that means you will be swallowing me whole!"

"What a stupid, ungrateful little fish you are!" cried the big fish. "I'm only swallowing you in order to protect you from all those nasty and dangerous things outside our world, little fish. I've already told you – I'm *not* going to eat you. I'll look after you in my tummy whilst I deal with the dangers outside. And don't forget I'm doing this *on your behalf!* *Noblesse oblige* and all that. We are stronger together don't you think?"

The big fish was by now very angry.

"Don't you see that I'm offering you protection in my tummy *and* fighting your enemies for you *and* giving you free parasites to eat *and* that I would be doing all this for you?"

The little fish was very sorry he had ever doubted the big fish. He knew he was too small and too weak to stand up to dangerous and nasty bullies outside, by himself. It would be so much better if he had the big fish as a friend who could fight on his behalf – and would also protect him in his tummy and give him his parasites to eat. Meekly, the little fish apologised to the big fish and agreed to the big fish's plans.

And that's how things turned out. The big fish went about his business, making the other inhabitants of the river very afraid, until eventually he became the most important animal in the river. The little fish was content in eating the parasites off the big fish's scales. Whenever danger appeared, the little fish would swim into the big fish's mouth and down into his belly. And then the big fish would fight against the danger and he would win. And because of his clean scales – thanks to the hard work of the little fish – he could swim faster and better than any of the other fish in the river.

Then the big fish decided that it would be good to have more little fishes to attend to his needs. So, he made many other little fishes join the first little fish in grooming his scales. The promises were the same – the little fishes were too small and too weak to defend themselves, so he, the big fish, would give them a welcome in his tummy if there was any danger and fight their enemies for them and supply them with the parasites. All the little fishes had to do in return was to keep the scales of the big fish in perfect condition and to recognise him as the sole owner of the river. Considering that the little fishes saw themselves as too small and too weak to defend themselves from outside threats and that they thought eating the parasites on the big fish's scales were a much more profitable venture than being eaten by the big fish himself, they agreed.

Now the big fish became even greedier. One day he saw a big morsel of food, in the middle of the river.

"Yummy" said the big fish, "I must have that to eat."

Now the little fishes had seen something like this before – they had, after all, lived in the river longer than the big fish. Some of them tried to warn the big fish that it was a trap, whilst others, still true to some ingrained belief of their independence before the big fish had come along, stayed quiet. They knew that whilst the big fish said he owned the river, there was in fact a two-legged animal, which never came into the water itself, which was even more powerful than the big fish – and it was even more dangerous to all the other animals in the river. This animal used all sorts of tricks, and the little fishes had been warned not to trust anything offered by the two legged animal.

The big fish did not listen to the little fishes who cried out their warnings. What did *they* know? They were only weak-minded, small, insignificant hangers on, compared to him – the big fish, who had supported them throughout, fought their battles for them and had lovingly protected them in his belly whenever there was a sign of danger. And the food was rightly his in any case as lord of the river.

Maybe the little fishes were a little jealous of only having had a diet of parasites off their lord's scales to eat for so long, never the really good food that the big fish regularly enjoyed. And it was *his* right to enjoy such good food.

"Envious, ungrateful, little fishes" muttered the big fish, and then his mouth seized the floating food.

The little fishes looked on. As they watched, they saw their lord being taken away from them. As his mouth covered the food, the little fishes saw that the big fish was being pulled upwards and upwards, further and further from them, towards the two legged creature and out of the river, forever. Some of the little fishes were sad at losing their lord and what he had given them. "He did *so* much for us!" exclaimed some of them. Then they added mournfully, "What are we going to do without him?" and started to cry.

The other little fishes smiled and started somersaulting with joy. These little fishes commented that they were no longer dependent on the whims of the big fish and no longer had to work unrecognised for their eating the parasites off his scales.

"We are free!" they shouted jubilantly. "We can control our own destinies now! We are no longer subservient to the big fish! No more do we fear that he could turn on us at any moment and eat us! Independence at last!"

The big fish was gutted that very night.

2 The little frogs and the big frogs

Once upon a time there lived a group of little frogs on a number of lily pads in the middle of a lake. The lily pads were comfortable, the sun was always shining and the frogs would croak to each other about how life was good. On top of that, the position of the lily pads and their pretty flowers ensured a good supply of flies. In essence then, the frogs considered themselves to be living in a demi-paradise.

And then one day, another group of frogs, much bigger than the first group came along. They had seen the potential of the lily pads and they wanted to claim them as their own. So the big frogs pushed the little frogs out, until the little frogs found themselves on far less attractive lily pads on the lake edge and having to wade through mud in order to eat, and to visit their fellows.

Then the big frogs offered a deal to the little frogs.

"You can come back to the clean, comfortable lily pads in the middle of the lake, if you learn how to croak like us," they said. "And you must not croak like you do now."

Some of the little frogs jumped at this idea. Did they really want to stay in a backwater of the lake with all its dirt and grime, little sunlight and far less abundance of flies? So they swam to the middle of the lake and soon they were croaking with new voice with the big frogs. They soon forgot about their old friends, the little frogs on the lake shore, and of course, they had no need to croak like they did with them. Croaking with the big frogs made them seem as if they were big frogs themselves – and indeed, they did well out of it. The lily pads were definitely better than those on the lake shore, the flies were indeed more numerous and the sun shone more brightly than in the shadier places where their erstwhile compatriots dwelt.

One of the little frogs became so important that he eventually became the chief of the big frogs. When some of the little frogs heard about this, they thought that as one of their number now controlled the lily pads again, it would be a good idea to 'reclaim their inheritance' as they put it. As a result, some of the more eager little frogs swam out to the middle of the lake, joined the big frog community and turned their backs forever on the group of little frogs.

One night, one of the big frogs heard a strange croaking coming from near the shore.

"It's those damn little frogs keeping me awake with their incessant, incomprehensible croaking!" he cried.

So he called forth a number of his fellow big frogs and together they swam to the little frogs' lily pads.

"How dare you croak in this barbarous way and keep us up at night!" thundered the big frog.

"We can't help it," said one of the little frogs meekly, "croaking like this is as natural as breathing to us."

"You *can* help it," shouted the big frog. "And I'm sure you're croaking about me too – and that according to the rules of our society in the middle of the lake is slander!"

"B-b-b-but ..." protested the little frog, but to no avail.

"Silence!" shouted the big frog. "You are one of the ringleaders in this devilish plot, I see. You will come with me to that old rotten log downstream where you will not be able to croak to anyone."

And that is how it turned out. Each time a little frog croaked in a way that the big frogs did not understand, they were escorted to the old rotten log. But this made some of the little frogs even more determined. Whilst some of them gave in and didn't want to suffer the harshness of being away from family and friends on the old rotten log, others continued croaking in the way their ancestors had done for centuries – even if that meant periods alone on the old rotten log and not able to croak to any of the other little frogs for some time. On their return to the lake side, these little frogs would go back to croaking in the same way as before.

Now the big frogs had control over the education of all the frogs in the lake. So the little frogs had to learn to croak in the same way as their teachers – who only croaked as the big frogs did. The little frogs found this difficult as they only croaked in the way of their parents and grandparents. So the big frogs devised a way of making their education system work. If they heard a little frog croaking, they would quickly pull the lily pad he was sitting on from under him and for a few seconds the little frog would think he was drowning. It was only if he had his wits about him and reacted very quickly, that the little frog could tread water and survive. The little frog students saw this event re-enacted so often that they quickly learnt that to avoid drowning or at least the sensation of drowning – which was just as scary – they should also learn to croak like the big frogs.

Sometimes, the big frogs held parties on their lily pads. On such occasions, they decided to invite the little frogs over for a few days and nights and share little pieces of bluebottle or dragonfly with them. But they would never give a *whole* insect to the little frogs – oh no! That just wasn't on! The little frogs should be pleased for any largesse on the part of the big frogs and wanting more was just being plain ungrateful.

One day, the little frogs found a new supply of insects for themselves. Inevitably, word got out to the big frogs in the middle of the lake and they sent a deputation to talk to the little frogs.

"We want your insects!" said one of the big frogs.

"Despite all that you have done for us – taken our lily pads, ensured that you have the best locations, made us croak like you do, nearly drowned our children for croaking naturally, taken our intellectual frogs to the old rotten log downstream and more, we will share them with you," replied the little frogs' representative, "but only on one condition – that you learn to croak like us."

"What impudent nonsense!" shouted the spokesfrog of the big frogs.

"But when you wanted us to be part of *your* community, you insisted that we forgot to croak like little frogs and to only croak like you as big frogs, didn't you?" queried the little frog, "What's the difference?"

"You all croak like us now!" retorted the big frog, "and croaking like a little frog is of no use to anyone."

"Well, it is to us" replied the little frog firmly. "It's as natural as breathing to *all* of us – you and me – to croak like we do, as you croak like you do. And you see, we wouldn't be able to take advantage of this new supply of insects without it. For as you know, only we little frogs know where they are to be had."

"Damn your croaking!" screamed the big frog. "We should have drowned all your young frogs when they were at school!"

"You very nearly did," replied the little frog softly. "But despite everybody and everything, we're still here! And unless you change tack, my friend – and we're only playing by your rules regarding this croaking business – we're keeping this secret supply of insects to ourselves."

The big frog growled and stomped away.

"I'll be back" he muttered, Terminator fashion.

3 The two men in the pub

Once upon a time there were two men sitting around a table in a pub. On the table there was a small tumbler with some golden coloured liquid inside.

"I say, old chap," said the first man pointing to the glass, "you seem to have a half empty glass of Scotch there. Let me top you up and dilute it for you with the best unionist water."

"Och nae, laddie," replied the second man. "Ta tae ye, a' the same. But thon glass is hauf fu' tae me. An' a dae like my whisky neat. I think I will get masel a double!"

4 Scottie and Jon Bull

Once upon a time, there lived in a town not so far away, a large fat man called Jon Bull. Jon Bull owned a little dog called Scottie. Every day, Jon Bull used to take Scottie for walks at the end of a tight leash. Then, they would come home, and he would open a tin of dog food and give it to Scottie. Scottie ate the food and stayed quiet. He remained faithful to his master.

Then one day, as Jon Bull and Scottie were walking in town with Scottie on his tight leash, they passed outside a butcher's shop. Inside the shop was a big, juicy bone.

"I want that bone," said Scottie, all of a sudden.

"What?" exclaimed Jon Bull. "You have a voice?

Scottie, you can speak?"

"Yes, I can," said Scottie, "and I've been quiet long enough."

"B-b-b-ut ...," stuttered Jon Bull, "why are you speaking now? Think of all that tinned dog food I've been giving you all these years – you don't need that bone. I've taken good care to give you food regularly. I've taken you for walks. I provide you with a nice warm home in which to live and sleep. And I do know what's good for you."

"Oh yes, you know what's good for me" retorted Scottie bitterly. "And as for the food, why, it's been the same old, bland dog food day in, day out. Sometimes it comes out of a red tin, another time it comes out of a blue tin. You've even tried deceiving me into thinking the new food – from a yellow and blue striped tin – is different. But quite frankly, Jon Bull, it's the same old recipe hashed up every time. And I'm sick to death of it."

"Why you impudent, ungrateful cur!" roared Jon Bull.

"All the other dogs have bones," replied Scottie, "I don't see why I should be any different. And you know as well as I do, the traditional image of a dog is with a bone between its teeth – not lapping away at some meat mixture in a bowl given to him rather condescendingly, I might add, by his master. I've seen it in the books you read."

"Fiddlesticks!" cried Jon Bull. "Are you trying to tell me, your master, how to look after my own dog – after all I've done for you?"

"Yes," said Scottie softly, "you might learn something from me."

"Such cheek!" blustered Jon Bull, his face reddening and his fat belly wobbling. "I've a good mind to thrash you, Scottie. Just because some mangy mongrels are allowed bones, you think you're entitled to some bones too! Well, I won't stand for it, do you hear? I'm your master and you're my dog – I tell you what to do, not the other way around!"

Scottie was not listening. He was obliged to get the resentments he had been feeling for years off his chest.

"And another thing," said Scottie, pursuing his argument calmly, "you say you've taken me for walks. Yes, you have – but always on your terms. The other dogs are left off the leash and are free to roam. You keep me on this tight leash, day in, day out. It's not normal."

Scottie thought by appealing to Jon Bull's ideas of fairness and the treatment which other dogs had that he would win the argument. He thought Jon Bull commended exercise, fresh air and freedom for dogs. What Scottie hadn't realised that these rules only applied to *other* dogs – not to him.

Jon Bull was having none of it.

"Not normal? Damn your impudence, Scottie! I

won't have you speak to me like that! You know full well that if I did let you off the leash, you couldn't possibly survive by yourself. You wouldn't get any food – you'd die of starvation. And you have a nice warm home with me. Enough of these ideas of freedom!"

Scottie was quiet for a bit. Jon Bull smirked. He had won the argument. He was right. He was always right. How dare that impudent, ungrateful puppy think that he knew best! I, Jon Bull, hold the leash. I, Jon Bull feed you well. I, Jon Bull give you a nice, warm home. What more could you possibly ask for, Scottie?

Some days later, Jon Bull and Scottie were in town again. Scottie was on his tight leash and they were walking past the butcher's shop again.

"I want that bone," said Scottie.

"We've had this conversation!" growled Jon Bull. "You're not getting it and that's final!"

Scottie weighed up his options. It was now or never. He bit Jon Bull hard on the ankle.

"Yyyeeeeooowww!" screamed Jon Bull, letting go of the leash.

This was the opportunity Scottie wanted – and he took it. He ran into the butcher's shop and onto the counter where the big juicy bone was. He could hear Jon Bull bellowing after him,

"Come back here, you ungrateful, vicious mutt!"

(Two possible scenarios to this story now present themselves. Which one is it to be? I leave the final decision to my readers).

Scenario 1

Having jumped onto the counter, Scottie surveyed the big, juicy bone. And then he sniffed it. He sniffed it again to check and then he realised, with bitter disappointment, that the bone did not smell very nice. It was not going to be very nice to taste either. Scottie's dreams were crushed and he sat on the counter with his head between his paws and cried his eyes out.

This gave Jon Bull the opportunity to recover his dog.

"Don't you ever run away from me again!" cried Jon Bull. "In fact, I've got the very thing to ensure that you will not."

Jon Bull proceeded to tighten the leash a couple of notches around Scottie's head.

"That should ensure your obedience in future," said Jon Bull. "Such a silly dog to have notions of juicy bones when he was fed so well at home by me."

"Was fed so well ... ?" whimpered Scottie through his tears.

"Oh yes" said Jon Bull maliciously, "you must be taught a thorough lesson for your behaviour, Scottie. And as for biting your master on the ankle – after all he has done for you – that is really beyond the pale."

Scottie gulped.

"Yes, my doggie friend, you will go back to your usual diet of tinned dog food. Only this time, I won't be quite as generous in my rations. You will live on half a tin a day – not your usual full tin. You understand don't you, Scottie? And in this period of economic austerity, you must appreciate I can't afford to give you a full tin every day, in any case. We must all make economic savings – we are all in this together!"

And goodness, how Scottie howled!

Scenario 2

Scottie surveyed and sniffed the big juicy bone.

"Mmmmmmmmmmmm," he sighed, "better than I expected. So much better than that boring, samey dog food I've been so used to getting from my master, Jon Bull."

And with that, Scottie seized the bone between his teeth – as he had seen so many other of his canine friends do in the past – and trotted out of the butcher's shop, his tail wagging furiously and happily. He was now just like them, a free doggie with his own bone, not attached by a tight leash and controlled by a surly master who always made all the decisions on Scottie's behalf. Scottie could look forward to a new life for himself – and one where he called all the shots.

Dear readers – which scenario is it to be for Scottie and Jon Bull?

The story concludes in September 2014.

5 Jock's birthday party

Jock was having a birthday. His Mummy and his Daddy wanted to ensure that he had the best birthday ever, so they made sure that they invited all of Jock's friends to the party. After playing a few games, the children were escorted to the table to eat. And goodness! There was *so* much to eat, and *so* much variety! Then it came to the desserts.

The children started on the big red jelly. But although they had been used to the big red jelly before at other birthday parties, this one didn't taste very nice. Maybe it was *too* big and had gone off – past its sell-by date, whispered some of the children.

Or maybe, as some other children thought, it had no taste at all – it was just a wobbly, bland, red mixture.

So the children decided to try the blue jelly. Oh no! *That* jelly was far too bitter to the taste! The children liked sweet things, and it was obvious that the blue jelly didn't fit the bill. All the children mentally made a solemn vow never to eat the blue jelly ever again.

The children decided to taste the yellow jelly. Now the yellow jelly was much smaller than the other jellies. But yuk! This jelly promised much but in fact had such a cloying taste that the children could not stand it – some were even sick after they had tasted it.

Some of the children thought that if they mixed the extremely sweet yellow jelly with the extremely bitter blue jelly, they would have a nicer dessert. But yuk and double yuk! This was actually the worst of all worlds – sometimes you could taste the bitterness of the blue jelly, and sometimes you could taste the excessive sweetness of the yellow jelly (although admittedly it was the bitterness of the blue jelly that tended to predominate). The children at Jock's birthday party hurriedly disposed of the new blue-yellow jelly in the rubbish bin.

And then they saw standing alone on the table, an impressive and resplendent golden ice cream with a dark chocolate sauce over it. They took up their spoons, and tentatively, knowing how they had been bitterly disappointed by the previous desserts, they started to sample the golden ice cream.

"Mmmmmmmmmmmm!" cried Jock.

"Yummy!" enthused Morag.

"Absolutely delicious!" added Hamish.

"I'm going to have some more of that!" said Catriona, scooping up a big spoonful of that lovely, creamy, golden ice cream.

And all the children agreed. The golden ice cream

was the best dessert they had ever had and Jock's party was the best they had ever attended too. They were sure to dance, play games and enjoy themselves more than ever before.

It was going to be the best party, ever!

6 The two clouds

Once upon a time, there were two clouds in the sky: One big dark cloud and one little fluffy white cloud. They were discussing who was the most important.

"Well, it's obviously me who's the most important," said the big dark cloud. "I can cover the whole sky and even block out the sun. I can cause rain to fall, and as a result, the crops of the people on Earth can grow. People respect me because I have a huge amount of talent: I can create rain, hail, sleet and snow. What can you ever hope to create like that?"

"Let's see," said the little white cloud. "I have no intention of covering the whole sky. I don't think it's such a good idea to block out the sun, in any case. How can you be so arrogant as to take a pride in that? The people on Earth want the sun to live by, and they are happy when they see he is out – and unhappy when you make him disappear. You say you have the power to cause rain to fall and cause crops to grow. This is true, but have you thought about this? When people are wet from your rain, they don't think about their crops – on the contrary, they think about how cold and wet and miserable they are from your rain. The same goes for your hail, sleet and snow. You have power, yes, but power to make people cold and miserable and even to freeze their crops which is not helping them at all, is it? And you can't even control your precipitations – if you rain too much, you cause further misery by causing flooding, damage to crops, hunger and disease. Your snow makes the people freeze to death too. People resent that. Are you proud of all that?"

"Bah, humbug!" growled the big, dark cloud. "What good are you to anyone? With your smallness you are no use at all. And as for your appearance ... Pah! Your soft, fluffy nature may appeal to those weak-minded romantics down there on Earth – but no one else! Completely impractical and unproductive, that's what you are! 'Wandering lonely as a cloud', indeed! Absolute pish!"

"You may have hit upon something there," conceded the little white cloud. "I may indeed be small – but this is to my advantage. I'm not a menace to other things like you are and my praises are sung on Earth. And that poetry you cited, it gives me some form of immortality, something you will never have."

The big dark cloud gave a loud rumble of thunder.

"Thank you for reminding me," said the little white cloud. "You also create thunder and lightning. That scares the wits out of the people on Earth. Is that also something to be proud of?"

"People are used to my presence," growled the big

dark cloud. "They don't want to change to something airy and light with no substance like you."

"I think you're wrong," said the little white cloud softly. "You never know, that come autumn 2014 people will be looking for the sun again – which, I dare suggest, is the normal state of affairs of people, in any case. How many people do you know actively go to places and seek *you* out, as opposed to me? I'll wager that come autumn 2014, I will be stronger than you and that it will be *me* making the weather!"

7 Of nations and shopkeepers

Once upon a time, there was a sleepy little village called Celtia. It was a very small place, and everyone knew each other and everyone was very friendly too. Celtia also had the usual little shops and its inhabitants would often go to these little shops to catch up on the latest village gossip and to exchange new ideas on a myriad of subjects. Amongst the most important shops in Celtia were Mr Scott's the Butcher's, Mr Jones's the Baker's and Mr Ayre's, who was the Candlestick maker.

Now as well as working for the common good of all the inhabitants of Celtia, the villagers also found time to relax and enjoy themselves of an evening. These evenings were often occasions of great festivity and fun – and were organised by the villagers of Celtia themselves for their own amusement. And they had talent too! Erin Ayre (Mr Ayre's daughter) was an accomplished fiddler. Mr Scott's brother-in-law, Douglas Mann, would regale the audience with his stories of motorcycling bravado and his own personal achievements aboard the 'iron horse.' Mr Jones's sister, Brittany, was a first rate player of the *binioù*. Occasionally, Mr Scott himself would join Erin and Brittany on the bagpipes and everyone agreed that they made wonderful music together.

The villagers of Celtia were very happy and their village thrived. There was room for everyone and everyone respected each other. But it was all a fool's paradise.

It was young Mr Trelawney (who was renowned in the village for his ice cream and pasties) who first noticed the change. He rushed into the local pub – the *Triskele* – one day and stammered out his message.

"They're building a massive supermarket just outside the village" he gasped breathlessly. "Smith's I think it's called. And I've just been attacked by one of their employees." He showed his black eye to the rest of the villagers.

After the villagers had given Mr Trelawney a drink and told him to calm down, they decided they had to start a campaign of some sort against this new, unwelcome supermarket. Mr Ayre, always one of the most fiery of the villagers wanted to 'punch the living daylights' out of Smith's Managing Director – even Mr Smith himself, if he ever got his hands on him. Couldn't the rest of them see that Smith's supermarket would suck the lifeblood out of Celtia and all their shops would close?

Mr Scott and Mr Jones however were more cautious. "We should write letters to Mr Smith. Petition him. Try and persuade him that we don't want his supermarket so close to Celtia."

Mr Ayre reluctantly agreed, muttering anti-Smith

threats under his breath. Events were soon to vindicate his approach. It became obvious that the softly-softly approach did not work – Smith's supermarket intended on growing and consequently to squeeze the local businesses. Mr Smith offered them shares in his enterprise and to buy them out – but they were too proud (or too stubborn) to accept.

"We're not getting anywhere" said Mr Ayre one day in the *Triskele*. "Smith is killing us – and all you lot are doing is writing petitions and wringing your hands. It's time for some direct action and for Smith to be taught a lesson!"

"It's only very slowly that one catches the hen," said Mr Jones.

Mr Ayre was not convinced. "Smith is laughing at us" he said. "I'm going to give Smith a punch up the bracket. Come on, Erin" and he seized his daughter's arm and marched out of the pub.

That very night, Mr Ayre carried out his threat and gave two black eyes to Mr Smith. The repercussions were serious – Mr Smith withdrew his share offer to the small shopkeepers and turned the screw tighter on the villagers of Celtia. Mr Trelawney's ice cream and pasty making business was completely taken over, so that that hapless man found himself with only a stall to himself within the colossus that was Smith's supermarket. Mr Scott and Mr Jones found they could only sell their meat and bread to Mr Smith (at a cheaper rate) and had to be grateful for lower profit margins. Only Mr Ayre stood apart, but even he, despite his resentments, found that Smith's had a monopoly position in selling candlesticks. (Many years later Smith's would sell their majority shareholding in Ayre's candlesticks business back to him – at a great profit to themselves, of course – whilst retaining the menorah making business for themselves).

And then recession hit the country. And it hit Celtia too, of course. Smith's supermarket went into difficulties and there was a grave fear amongst its employees that the company would be wound up.

Will Smith's supermarket dissolve in the current climate? Would Mr Scott's nerve hold when he demanded that his shareholding in the company be paid back – at full market value? Would Mr Jones have the confidence in insisting the same for himself – when the time arose? And would poor young Mr Trelawney get a proper job for himself and no longer to be considered a remote outpost of the Smith retail empire?

Watch this space ...

8 The four balloons

Once upon a time, there were four balloons at a party. There was the big, red balloon who thought he was the most important balloon there – he had been going to parties for as long as he could remember, and he thought of himself as the partygoers' natural choice of balloon. He floated silently over the more recently arrived partygoers, but was rather startled when one of them gave him a large smack across his big, red face with the palm of his hand. In his shock, the big, red balloon floated too close to the radiator ... until ... BBBAAANNNGGG! The big, red balloon exploded. Most of the partygoers didn't seem to notice however and they carried on dancing. Others gave a loud cheer – these little, local events adding to the general feeling of mirth at the party. It would take a long time to find a replacement big, red balloon.

The blue balloon hardly ever got a look in at parties. This was because she was very difficult to inflate. No matter how much one huffed and puffed, more hot air seemed to come *out* of the wee blue balloon than ever went in. The partygoers eventually decided that it wasn't worth the effort to try and inflate the blue balloon, so they left her in the corner to wither away and become wrinkled and unloved.

The yellow balloon was a much smaller balloon than the red and blue balloons. However, when one inflated him, one felt sure that he promised to be just as big and as good looking as the big, red balloon. Sadly though, this was very much only for show. Further, the partygoers had forgotten to tie a knot in the yellow balloon's neck. As a result, he escaped from their grasp and spluttered all over the room, expelling hot air as he went.

"Pppppppppppppppuuuuuhhhhhhffffffffffffff," said the yellow balloon, coming to land side by side alongside the dishevelled blue balloon.

And now we come to the gold and black balloon. The partygoers were initially suspicious of balloons which had two colours. The gold and black balloon took some time to be inflated. But when he did – he looked magnificent! The partygoers gave him the thumbs up as the smartest balloon in the party and they started to strike him gently with their hands – batting him to and fro between their friends. The gold and black balloon was in his element – he had become the balloon of choice for partygoers everywhere. The gold and black balloon was exceedingly happy and he was making the partygoers happy too. This was a win-win situation and everyone knew it.

It was going to be the best party ever!

9 The two books

Once upon a time, there were two books for sale side by side in a bookshop – a big, hefty encyclopaedia, and by his side, a much smaller, but more colourful encyclopaedia. Customers regularly came into the shop and flicked through the books before moving on and going about their business.

One quiet day, the two encyclopaedias found themselves alone with no customers looking through their pages, so they decided, to relieve the monotony, to chat to each other. The subject of the conversation, perhaps inevitably, was a comparison between their respective values and worth and which one of them the bookshop's customers would eventually buy.

"They are sure to buy me," said the big encyclopaedia, puffing out his great papery chest. "I have a long history behind me. I was first published in 1707 and I hold a wealth of factual material between my covers. People have used my previous editions as *the* definitive source of information for many, many years. What use are you to anyone as an encyclopaedia? You can't possibly compete with my track record. And your smallness militates against you – how can you possibly have as much information between your covers as me?"

"Yes, I agree that I am much smaller than you are," replied the little encyclopaedia, "but I have many advantages that you don't have. I'm smaller, so more compact in my outlook and can concentrate on what readers consider key events, instead of glossing over them like you do. My smallness makes me user friendly too. You're just an old, heavy tome that is decidedly unwieldy. Additionally, I provide links to websites so that readers can follow up their reading in other places –

can you do that?"

The big encyclopaedia was silent.

"My cover is colourful and vibrant, whilst yours is grey and uninspiring," went on the little encyclopaedia.

"People like something that they are used to," mumbled the big, heavy encyclopaedia. "I've provided them with knowledge since 1707 – and people respect my authority on encyclopaedic matters. They have no need to reference other sources like this new-fangled Enternutty thing or whatever you call it."

"It's the Internet," replied the little encyclopaedia.

The big encyclopaedia looked puzzled.

"It's part of the World Wide Web" explained the little encyclopaedia patiently.

The big encyclopaedia frowned and said nothing.

"I see you already have gaps in your knowledge

which I am in a position to fill. It rather proves my point about me being contemporary too." The little encyclopaedia had the wind in his pages or the bit between his covers now (he knew both expressions, of course). "And another thing, you say that you were first published in 1707?" he went on.

The big, heavy encyclopaedia nodded. "Yes, indeed, you young whippersnapper. And I'm proud of it!" And I'm proud of my history too!" he said.

"Well," said the little encyclopaedia, "things have moved on since then. And I don't see much reflection of those things between your pages. I don't think any prospective reader could possibly take you seriously if your starting off point is always going to be 1707!"

"Bah, humbug!" growled the big encyclopaedia. "I've got very big sections on Empires under 'E' and Unionism under 'U'. There's also a big feature on colours – Red, White and Blue all have large paragraphs to themselves. People enjoy reading these things."

"Yes, I had noticed that," replied the little encyclopaedia. "There are also two big articles on England under 'E' and the United Kingdom under 'U' on your pages. I'm surprised you didn't actually bring those two articles together ..." The little encyclopaedia gave a sad smile.

The big encyclopaedia gave a smirk. "My editors almost did," he said. "And you remember my cousin, Britannica. He had 'Wales, See England.'" The big encyclopaedia was puffing out his large, papery chest again. "You will see a cross-reference at the end of the article on England to 'see also Great Britain, United Kingdom.'"

"But you contain so little information about Scotland under 'S' and Wales under 'W'" went on the little encyclopaedia. "And nothing under 'C' for Cornwall. These are serious lacunae in a well-respected encyclopaedia, as you are wont to call yourself."

The big encyclopaedia had nothing to say. He slammed himself shut and the conversation ended.

Which encyclopaedia will *you* choose? Will it be the old, dusty, unwieldy, grey, not user friendly and out of date one? Or will you buy the smaller, more compact, student friendly, colourful encyclopaedia containing the more up to date information and containing links to other exciting references via the World Wide Web and other resources?

It's up to you – you, the book buying public of Scotland – to decide which encyclopaedia to buy.

10 The house that Jack built

Once upon a time, a man called Jack decided to build a house. He collected together some white bricks and started to lay the foundations to his house. But he was not happy with just white bricks, so he found some black bricks and mortared them beside the white bricks. And then he found some red bricks and placed them into the west wing of his house, and then some blue bricks which he placed in the north wing and finally, some green bricks.

Jack's house was now built and he stood back to admire his handiwork. He was very happy with his efforts. But something seemed to be missing. Yes, that was it. All those different colours were rather jarring to the eye. He should try to minimise their effect – create some sort of uniformity.

Jack thought first he should paint the whole house white. Then he had second thoughts. A neighbour, not too far down the road had already called his place 'The White House' and Jack did not wish to offend his neighbour. The man was known to get angry very quickly, was generally irritable and for ever meddling in other peoples' affairs. It was best to keep on the right side of his neighbour, not to cross him thought Jack. So Jack dismissed the idea of painting his own house completely white.

Then Jack thought that uniformity was best applied by painting his house all over in red, white and blue. That would effectively submerge the black and green bricks, and the blue and red bricks would think – mistakenly, of course – that they had some role in the great design that was the house that Jack built. The white bricks of course were very happy – being more numerous in the first place, they could easily assimilate themselves with the new paint. And so it was that Jack painted his house red, white and blue. He called his new home, 'Union House' and he was very pleased with all that he had achieved.

And then, one, dark night, there was a very violent thunderstorm outside. Union House shook in the wind and the roof creaked. Jack was a little afraid and had very little sleep that night.

When Jack got up the following morning, the first thing he did was to survey the damage. He noticed that the rain had washed off much of the red, white and blue paint from the front of the house. The green bricks were now visible again. Worse, some (but not all) of the green bricks had become loose and were now scattered about all over the garden. The blue and red bricks had also reappeared, but at least they were still attached to the house. There seemed to be little damage to the south wing of the house where the white bricks were. In fact, it was hard to tell where their whiteness ended and the white of the red, white and blue paint started. Anyway, the upshot was this – the house had *not* collapsed in the storm, despite the damage to some of the green bricks, Jack reapplied the red, white and blue paint to the remaining house bricks (he had however less paint this time, and he was also a little less careful than previously, so if you looked carefully, you could see the original blue, red or black brick standing out.)

Now all the professional seismologists were convinced that the area on which Jack's house was located was an area particularly prone to earthquakes. Indeed, there had been a few rumbles noted after the violent thunderstorm we mentioned earlier – but Jack had taken very little notice of these. They did however cause the red, white and blue paintwork to peel a little more. As a result, the original blue, red and black bricks had become more and more visible.

The seismologists were further convinced that a very large earthquake was imminent – or at least within the next two years. They advised Jack to leave Union House as they feared that when (*not* 'if') such an event occurred, it was exceedingly likely that Union House would be completely destroyed and that Jack himself would be found under its rubble.

Jack was in a quandary. He didn't want to believe the seismologists or any other experts. And he didn't want to leave Union House. Yet he was fearful that if all the prognostics were correct, he would become a casualty in his own home when the earthquake came and Union House collapsed around his ears. The build up to the earthquake was proving to be very exciting.

11 The three trees

Scene: A clearing in a wood. Two lean, young trees standing side by side. Facing them is a taller, older looking tree with slightly careworn bark. It seems as if they are having an animated conversation. Let's listen in.

First lean, young tree (addressing the taller, older tree): Good morning, Brother. We are elders of our Church and we want to tell you about Jesus Christ.

Second lean, young tree (helpfully): That's *elders*, Brother and not *alders*. A lot of people mix us up. But they're a totally different sect to us.

Older tree: I'm afraid you're barking up the wrong tree with me, my son. I could say you're barking, full stop, but that would be a very un-Christian thing to say.

The two young trees say nothing.

Older tree (drawing himself up to his full height): You do know who I am, don't you? (Pause) Don't you recognise me?

Pause of about a minute. The two young trees look at each other in puzzlement. They look at the older tree and then at each other again. They are completely at a loss.

Second lean, young tree: I'm afraid you've got us stumped, Sir. Who are you?

Older tree (sighing): Dear boy. My name is Rowan. I used to be the Archbishop of Canterbury. Consequently, I was the leader of quite a few followers of Jesus Christ worldwide. I believe my roots are much deeper than yours too.

The two younger trees, although elders, fall silent(ly).

12 The caterpillar grows up

Once upon a time, there was a little caterpillar. He was considered by a lot of the other animals to be a small, ugly little creature.

"How I wish I was free and beautiful like you," he said one day to the butterflies. "Free to fly in the warm air currents, away from these bullying creatures who poke fun at my smallness and ugliness."

"You will, little caterpillar," said one of the butterflies, giving a tinkling laugh. "You will, one day soar with us in the deep air oceans and we will welcome you as one of us. We'll also look after you and love you as one of our own."

"Oh thank you, thank you" gushed the little caterpillar, who had never been loved or appreciated so much before in his life. "I certainly hope so."

"Believe in yourself," said one of the wisest butterflies. "Believe in better."

Suddenly, a large, black shadow materialised in the sky. The butterflies fled in all directions all a-flutter.

"Aha! What have we here?" cackled a big white bird.

The caterpillar gulped.

"By rights, I should eat you," said the big white bird. "But you're far too small and far too ugly for my taste. Be gone with you – before I change my mind."

The caterpillar gulped again. "T-t-t-thank you" he stuttered.

"Don't mention it!" said the big white bird and flew off, cackling.

Now the little caterpillar was a good little caterpillar. He ate all his greens – just like his Mummy caterpillar told him to. In fact, he ate *so* much that he felt very sleepy. So creeping inside his gold and black cocoon, he fell into a deep and contented sleep.

He dreamt of the free butterflies and then dreamt – a nightmare – of the big white bird gobbling him up.

In the morning, the caterpillar woke up inside his gold and black cocoon. Only he was not a caterpillar any more. He was a beautiful blue and white butterfly.

The small, ug-..., sorry, the beautiful new blue and white butterfly spread his wings and joined the other butterflies in the sky.

"Welcome!" said the wise butterfly who had told him to believe in himself the day before. "We told you you could do it!"

"Yes! Yes! And thank you. Thank you, all" said the blue and white butterfly, smiling.

It was such a joyous feeling – freedom and having the love and respect of the other butterflies, in the clear blue sky. He was free of all those nasty bullies too who had previously mocked him for his size and appearance.

He had all those lovely, pretty flowers which he hadn't seen before to visit too. Life was very good and the blue and white butterfly had found his place at last. He was very happy.

13 The two suitcases

Once upon a time, there were two suitcases lying side by side on a bed, waiting to be packed. The first suitcase was an old, sturdy but quite battered one. It had obviously seen better days and both its exterior and its interior were now decidedly the worse for wear. Its outside covering bore witness to the many knocks it had suffered on its travels and its corners were badly scuffed. The first suitcase's hinges squeaked when you opened and closed the lid. All over the outer surface of the first suitcase were labels of where the suitcase had visited – India, Jamaica, South Africa and Australia to mention but four. By now, these labels had started to peel away, giving the suitcase an even more drab appearance.

Now, previously, the old suitcase had four fully functioning wheels. However, if one examined it in more detail, and rolled it, one could see that, in fact, one of the wheels was out of synch. with the other three – wonky, I think is the expression. It would only be a matter of time before this wheel detached itself completely from the battered old suitcase: the wheel had lost three out of the four screws holding it in place. To compound the general shabby appearance of the first suitcase, it was clearly visible that two of the other three wheels had also lost screws, resulting in further wonkiness. In consequence, the suitcase's owner found it extremely difficult to steer the suitcase properly or to maintain it on a straight and forward trajectory for any length of time.

In contrast, the second suitcase seated beside the first on the bed looked a decidedly new model. It bore no scuff marks, no dents and had a definite modern and contemporary feel to it. Its plush blue and white interior was resplendent and this appeared to invite the installation of any discerning holidaymaker's clothes and other items. The second suitcase did not as yet bear any stickers denoting previous foreign excursions, but one could almost palpably feel its anticipation of receiving them – all by now manufactured from eco-friendly paper unlike the non-recyclable material which was peeling off the older suitcase's labels.

Whereas the first suitcase's combination lock – 1707 – did not always succeed in fully closing that suitcase firmly and securely (a faulty mechanism was blamed by some), the second suitcase's combination lock – 2014 – when activated, resulted in a highly satisfying "CLACK" of the suitcase. In consequence, the holidaymaker's clothes and any other items of value inside the suitcase were protected thoroughly and securely from the threat of theft from outside. It was clear therefore that the first suitcase's ability to deter thieves and secure the holidaymaker's assets was severely compromised because of its defective system.

Which suitcase are *you* going to take with you as you embark on your great adventure in exploring new unexplored areas, Scottish holidaymaker? Is it to be the clapped out, creaky, not fully functioning and non-theft proof suitcase with the wonky wheels? Or will you choose the sleek, new, modern suitcase with the secure combination lock – a suitcase indeed that can justifiably hold its head up high when it joins the other suitcases on the airport carousel?

14 The two traffic lights I

There were once two traffic lights – one red traffic light and one green traffic light. (A third traffic light – a yellow one located between the two was considered so insignificant that he doesn't merit any further commentary.) The red and green traffic lights performed their usual functions and the vast majority of motorists only gave them a cursory glance to ensure their safe passage in the humdrum of their daily lives.

However, one day the red traffic light and the green traffic light decided to engage each other in a discussion about their respective merits and their worth amongst the motorists.

"My great value," said the red traffic light, "is that people have always obeyed my signal. I make them stop and wait for my further orders. I stop the motorists from going ahead to their destination too quickly. And as I am always on top of the traffic signal, it is to me that motorists look first for guidance."

"How arrogant you are!" exclaimed the green traffic light. "You think you get motorists' obedience because you tell them to stop. People obey you because they have no choice. They might be afraid that you will never change – but change you must."

"Pah!" harrumphed the red traffic light, "and I suppose you're the motorists' friend!"

"Well," said the green traffic light evenly, "I don't claim to have all the answers – unlike you – but I can tell you this. I never impede the motorists' progress. On the contrary, I facilitate them reaching their goal much quicker than you do. I allow them to move forward and not to be snarled up in a long, boring traffic jam like you do so often."

The red traffic light had nothing to say. He realised that he had to change at some point and it seemed as if the green traffic light had all the answers.

Am I right in thinking that you – the motoring public of Scotland also agree with the green traffic light? And that you too wish to arrive at your destination fresh and excited to make new discoveries? That you do not wish to be thwarted in this by some stubborn, arrogant and controlling red traffic light? I certainly do hope so – they do seem to be the most natural things in the world to want.

15 The two traffic lights II

There were once two traffic lights – one red traffic light and one green traffic light. (A third traffic light – a yellow one located between the two was considered so insignificant that he doesn't merit any further commentary.) The red and green traffic lights performed their usual functions and the vast majority of motorists only gave them a cursory glance to ensure their safe passage in the humdrum of their daily lives.

However, one day, the red traffic light and the green traffic light decided to engage each other in a discussion about their respective merits and their worth amongst the motorists.

"My great value," said the red traffic light, "is that people have always obeyed my signal. I make them stop and wait for my further orders. I stop the motorists from going ahead to their destination too quickly. And as I am always on top of the traffic signal, it is to me that motorists look first for guidance."

"How arrogant you are!" exclaimed the green traffic light. "You think you get motorists' obedience because you tell them to stop. People obey you because they have no choice. They might be afraid that you will never change – but change you must."

"Pah!" harrumphed the red traffic light, "and I suppose you're the motorists' friend!"

"Well," said the green traffic light evenly, "I don't claim to have all the answers – unlike you – but I can tell you this. I never impede the motorists' progress. On the contrary, I facilitate them reaching their goal much quicker than you do. I allow them to move forward and not to be snarled up in a long, boring traffic jam like you do so often."

The red traffic light had nothing to say. He realised that he had to change at some point and it seemed as if the green traffic light had all the answers.

Am I right in thinking that you – the motoring public of Wales also agree with the green traffic light? And that you too wish to arrive at your destination fresh and excited to make new discoveries? That you do not wish to be thwarted in this by some stubborn, arrogant and controlling red traffic light? I certainly hope so – they do seem to be the most natural things in the world to want.

16 The boxing match

There's an engrossing boxing match taking place at the moment in the Britannia Stadium. Let's go over and see what's happening. It's proving to be an exciting bout with the old, experienced champion, George Britten, in the red, white and blue shorts, trying to retain his crown from the challenger, Jock Scott in the blue and white shorts.

The first three or four rounds have gone the old Champion's way. His experience seems to have outshone that of his challenger, and he has landed a number of punches to Jock Scott's body. Under his new trainer – known for his gold and black suit, and called Nat – Scott has learnt how to trade a few blows with George Britten, but over those first few rounds, has not inflicted that much damage. Elizabeth Britten would have been proud of her boy. A little jab from Scott early on – known as the McIntyre – initially irritated the Champion, but Britten soon shrugged it off.

A few rounds later however, and it can be seen that Scott was beginning to gain in confidence from the fact that Britten has not succeeded in knocking him out. A quick upper cut to the chin – Scott's trademark 'Ewing punch' – comes out of nowhere and stunned the Champion. Soon, Britten was on the ropes and Scott tried to press home his advantage. The boxers were locked together and, with Scott aiming for the winning punch, the referee shouted out "Break!" and stepped in to divide them. (Scott would later complain that the referee had ordered them to break too early – he was ahead on points and about to deliver his winning punch.)

The longer the boxing match went on, the older Champion became more and more sluggish. He started receiving blows and cuts at the hands of his much younger Challenger and his cauliflower ear became more and more noticeable. It was then that Britten decided to change his tactics. He began to hit below Scott's belt – a highly dubious, if not illegal boxing move. Luckily, the referee saw this and awarded the round to Scott, warning Britten that if he did it again he would be disqualified. This enraged Britten further and he started to up his illegal behaviour; behaviour which was not always visible to the referee but which had Scott's supporters in the crowd when they saw it shouting at the inadequacies of the referee.

And now you join us in the last but one round of this enthralling contest. Britten, the reigning Champion is clearly flagging, whilst his young Challenger, Scott, looks on the top of his game. You could say, he's running rings round his older opponent. Britten's second, Cameron, is looking increasingly anxious and may be tempted to throw in the towel at any time. And now Scott throws a heavy Salmond punch which has the Champion reeling. Britten falls to the floor, completely disorientated. He struggles to his feet, and takes the mandatory standing eight count. It looks like curtains for Britten.

How long will it be before Scott delivers the knockout blow?

17 *S.S. Anglia*

There was once a large steam ship of the name *S.S. Anglia*. She was the largest steam ship of her class, and the pride of her Line, the Britannic Line. More often than not, she was painted out in the Britannic Line colours, red, white and blue and she was instantly recognisable when she was on the high seas. In fact, *S.S. Anglia* was very often on the high seas and she had taken on all sorts of different cargo: spices from India, bananas from the Caribbean, and less talked about amongst the Britannic Line's Board of Directors, slaves from Africa. All these made the Britannic Line a very successful shipping Line, and the directors of the company became very rich men. (These were people who no one really knew much about, only that they raked in obscene profits.) There was barely a port in the world that had not had a visit from *S.S. Anglia* – from the Falkland Islands to Gibraltar, from Auckland in New Zealand to the Cape of Good Hope via Aden and Bombay; *S.S. Anglia* had been to them all.

One day, *S.S. Anglia* was preparing herself once more in her home port to go on a voyage to a far-flung territory where the Britannic Line's directors had an interest. As she was sailing out of the port, she came across three little merchant vessels who had come to see her off. Their names were *M.V. Alba*, *M.V. Cambria* and *M.V. Kernow*. *S.S. Anglia* towered over these three merchant vessels, and if they had not been careful, they would have been swamped by *S.S. Anglia*'s wake.

"Hey, be careful!" yelled *M.V. Alba*, "you could have submerged us all!"

"So sorry!" shouted *S.S. Anglia* back cheerfully, not really meaning it. "I can't stay and chat to you little boats. Things to do, cargoes to acquire, people to see. You know how it is? Oh, of course, you don't, do you? Poor little weak, insignificant, parochial merchant vessels!" *S.S. Anglia* chuckled. "What good are you to anyone?"

"Yeah, yeah," said *M.V. Cambria*, "we know you don't care a fig about us. Not even after all we've done for you!"

"What have you *ever* done for me?" asked *S.S. Anglia* scornfully.

"Well ... ," began *M.V. Cambria*, but *M.V. Alba* interrupted her. *M.V. Alba* was rather more confident in speaking to *S.S. Anglia* than the other merchant vessels – the others were rather in awe of *S.S. Anglia* and often let *M.V. Alba* lead and speak on their behalf. This was not really good for *M.V. Cambria* or *M.V. Kernow*'s self-confidence, but at least they knew they had a good friend in *M.V. Alba*.

"What *M.V. Cambria* is trying to say, is that she supplied you with all the coal to convert into steam which powers your voyages. In addition, I, *M.V. Alba* helped to deliver the iron and steel that made you in the first place. And also the steam boilers that power you were carried by me when you were being built."

"And I carried the tin from which your whistle is made," piped up *M.V. Kernow*, not wishing to be left out.

"Pish! Tush!" exclaimed *S.S. Anglia*. "As I said, I've got far more important things to do than stand around, chattering to the likes of you! Look at you all, stuck in this backwater harbour, plying your parochial trade on the same stretch of water, day in, day out. You should get out more – see the world! Just like I do. Travel does *so* broaden one's horizons, don't you think?" *S.S. Anglia* laughed, a deep, sarcastic laugh. "I'm sure that I carry more cargo than all three of you put together too!" she said, after she had stopped laughing.

And then with a loud blast on her whistle – the one that *M.V. Kernow* had help deliver – *S.S. Anglia* steamed out of the harbour.

Now, as so often happens, nemesis is the partner of hubris. That day, *S.S. Anglia* had a new skipper aboard – Captain Cameron. It was said that Captain Cameron had had very little training in seamanship, maybe he had steered the odd raft on Lake Oxford or in his youth had toyed with a radio controlled catamaran on Eton Water – both renowned for being shallow stretches of water which often evaporated completely in high summer owing to the strength of the sun. Be that as it may, Captain Cameron of the *S.S. Anglia* had very little navigational skills and even less of the complicated mechanisms involved in setting up the autopilot. This he confidently (but misguidedly, as it turned out) entrusted to his second in command, Commander Clegg. (There were some of Captain Cameron's crew who thought that this position should have been assigned to First Mate Osborne – and had threatened to mutiny over this – but, for the time being, Captain Cameron had managed to keep the mutineers in check. It is of course highly debatable whether First Mate Osborne could have averted the tragedy that befell *S.S. Anglia* later, had he been in charge of the autopilot. Stoker Johnson watched and followed these developments with interest from his own boiler room, downstairs. However, he didn't throw in his hand with the putative mutineers – at least not just then. He kept his own counsel and kept on shovelling the coal that powered *S.S. Anglia*. What is clear however is that culpability for the ensuing accident to *S.S. Anglia* extended top-down and all the crew were to be held accountable for their actions and omissions on that fateful day.)

But we are jumping ahead of ourselves a little. We had left *S.S. Anglia*, steaming happily out of harbour, leaving *M.V. Alba*, *M.V. Cambria* and *M.V. Kernow* bobbing uncertainly in the waves caused by her wake. Suddenly, there was an almighty crash. Knowing the local seas much longer than *S.S. Anglia* or her crew, the three merchant vessels immediately knew what had happened – *S.S. Anglia* had collided with a sandbank, located just outside the mouth of the harbour. They looked on in amazement as *S.S. Anglia*, the pride of the Britannic Line which had so recently dwarfed them, now faced them, looking completely stricken and listing outrageously to starboard. (That's leaning extremely to the right, for you landlubbers.)

The three merchant vessels decided as one that they should steam to *S.S. Anglia*'s aid. Bravely they sailed towards the stricken vessel and succeeded between them in rescuing all the crew of the *S.S. Anglia*, including Captain Cameron himself. Some thought that it would have been far better had they not saved the Captain, but the merchant vessels' argument was not really with ordinary individuals, but rather with the Britannic Line and all the cargoes that had been commissioned (often illegally, too – like the slaves) to be carried by its ships, for the exclusive benefit and profit of the Britannic Line's Board of Directors.

However, although Captain Cameron and his crew had been heroically saved by *M.V. Alba*, *M.V. Cambria* and *M.V. Kernow* between them, (who, quite rightly, basked in the glory of being in the right place at the right time for once – and could claim the individual credit for their acts of bravery and selflessness; something which *S.S. Anglia* usually often took credit for for herself instead of them), the Captain and his crew would now have to face another ordeal: a court martial. At that court martial, all the members of the *S.S. Anglia*'s crew were found guilty of gross misconduct and negligence and were dismissed from the employ of the Britannic Line. Captain Cameron lost his commission, with a note from the court martial that he should never be entrusted to command any sea-going vessel again.

It was a cruel irony according to some, that on the *very* day these judgements were pronounced, *S.S. Anglia* herself sank beneath the waves; waves that she had ruled for many a long year for the benefit of the Britannic Line. The hope and the glory that was the Britannic Line were also over.

18 Meet the Brittens – A dysfunctional family like no other

Once upon a time, there lived a rather big family called the Brittens in a small, detached house all to themselves. As the house was small and the family big, it was natural there would be some tensions within the household. This is to be expected of any family. But the Brittens were a special case. There was regular bickering with diverging attitudes and opinions held by the different members of the family.

George Senior was the father of the family and so, inevitably the Head of the household. It was his job at home, not very successfully, one might add, to try and maintain discipline in the house. His sons, of whom more presently, often had conflicting needs and interests, and George Senior was not always best placed to respond to them. He did however have a favourite amongst them, George Junior, who he hoped, would one day, continue doing the same job as he did – he was a rather self-important paperclip clerk at YooKay Ltd. – and inherit his father's expertise. George Senior was a firm believer in primogeniture. The idea of partible inheritance where *all* his sons would inherit equal shares in the property he owned was both alien and anathema to him.

Helping him in trying to maintain control in the household was George Senior's wife. She was a woman of mystery, and people knew very little about her – even her name was unknown. In the family, she was known simply as Mother, and revered for having some sort of mystical presence – at least by George Senior and George Junior. She pretended to herself, like her husband, that she managed the household well, but in reality, she often neglected her other sons, Jock, Dai, Piran and Mick/Mike and gave most of her love and affection to George Junior.

George Junior was a strapping lad, a chip off the old block as far as his father was concerned and he tended to dominate his siblings. In fact, he resembled his father so much, in appearance, mannerisms and mentality, that strangers in town often mistook one for the other. George Senior and George Junior could almost have passed for identical twins! He was also his mother's favourite and as previously mentioned, his father had high hopes of him inheriting the role of chief paperclip clerk at 'Uncle' Sam Washington's subsidiary company, YooKay Ltd. George Junior – like all his brothers – paid rent to his parents for staying in their house, but he was convinced that he paid more rent than they did. They did not pay their way as much as he did. And it was they who would do most of the squabbling and bickering – not him, not cool, calm, phlegmatic George Junior. He had even taught this attitude to his own father, George Senior, when the latter had despaired at the latest outbreak of tantrums from Jock and Dai. George's attitude towards his brothers however was ambivalent. On the one hand, when he heard that Jock wanted to leave, he was immediately distressed – but only in a selfish way. He thought he wouldn't be able to plunder Jock's stock of dirty magazines, nor play on his computer again if Jock left. At the same time, he knew that if Jock *did* leave the family home, he, George Junior, would receive more attention again and more preferential treatment from his parents.

Jock, as may have been noted, was the most rebellious of the family. Not for him the staid, cramped little detached house. He wanted out. He wanted to see the world for himself. And he wanted to stand on his own two feet. As a result, he was the main catalyst of rows between himself and George Junior, and with his parents, George Senior and Mother. He believed he paid his way in rent as well as anyone else in the household and was annoyed when all his achievements were credited to George Junior instead. As a toddler, Jock had often spoken to himself in a form of gibberish that no one else understood. George Senior and Mother, however, were very pleased to see that with their disciplined approach – usually by delegating their maid, Mhairi Crochaid, to use a stick on the lad – that this gibberish was beaten out of Jock and that he grew out of it. They were less successful with Dai, as will be seen later. Jock also had a girlfriend/boyfriend of long-standing, Francis Farr.

Francis Farr was born as a girl, under the name of Frances Near. She and Jock met at the local primary school and they instantly fell in love. Whether it was the mutual interest in wearing skirts that attracted them, I don't know. All I do know is that they instantly showed an affinity for each other. Their love blossomed throughout the school period and they eventually became engaged.

This position became intolerable to the older members of the Britten family. George Senior railed against their Alliance, Mother tut-tutted and George Junior was mad with envy. George Junior had even had designs on Frances himself and he couldn't bear that he had been outwitted – and that by a member of his own family. He did his utmost to break Jock and Frances's engagement, all to no avail.

And then, something quite singular happened. Frances had a breakdown. As a result of this breakdown, she was never the same girl again. In fact, she was never a girl again. Convincing herself that her coy, soft, femininity was actually a disadvantage, Frances decided on a sex-change. The only way to succeed was to become more bullish, more mannish, more aggressive. So Frances Near turned into Francis Farr. (The change in surname too was to underline the distancing between Jock and herself/himself.) Francis, in order to prove his new masculinity soon decided to flex his muscles and started showing domineering signs of his own – just like the two Georges. He was particularly overbearing to his own family, notably his cousin, Britney.

Jock was in shock initially from the double whammy – he had lost his girlfriend. And she had now become a he. Could Jock still love her/him as previously? Jock took a long time to think. Frances/Francis now lived on Europe Street, flanked on either side by Jerry Berlin and Diego Madrid. Jock knew that the situation in the Britten household was unbearable – George Junior was now mocking him regularly for losing his girlfriend. What was Jock to do? Did he have the courage of his convictions to stride out of the Britten household and set himself up, all by himself, on Europe Street, not too far away from his love? He did after all still maintain strong feelings for Frances/Francis and he didn't want to lose her/his friendship at least – a source of strength when things got tough in the Britten household. Jock pondered the questions long and deep. He was unsure of what to do. "Should I leave or should I go?" the thought churned in his head incessantly.

Now let us return to the other members of the

Britten family. Below Jock in the pecking order came Dai. Dai was a strange boy. He was often very placid and quiet – but not in the same way as his father and George Junior. He admired the way that Jock stood up to their parents and answered George Junior back. Dai was also sure that he respected Jock for wanting to leave the detached house where they lived – but was not brave enough (or old enough, perhaps) to take that step himself. George Junior would find this – and many other things of Dai's a great source of mirth: Dai was a coward or Dai interested himself in "girly, weedy pursuits," like poetry and folk dancing, George Junior would say. Dai then retreated into his shell and would say nothing.

Dai could also be found as often or not, talking some fantastic gibberish to himself which nobody else in the family understood. George Senior and Mother, empowered by the success they had had in beating such gibberish out of Jock, decided on the same approach with Dai. In this however, they were less successful. Although Dai did eventually learn to speak English, he would continue to prattle these unintelligible words whenever he could. The teachers at Dai's school also tried to beat it out of him – inflicting deep physical and psychological scars as a result – but Dai never fully gave up on his 'secret language.' It would be much later, upon entering secondary school, that more enlightened teachers would converse with Dai and that he felt more comfortable with them than he had at home. As a result, Dai's examination marks also improved substantially and his self-confidence grew.

Who else was a member of this dysfunctional family of Brittens? Well, there was baby Piran, who was only just learning to speak and crawl by himself. Being the youngest, Piran was subjected to all the teaching resources that George Senior and Mother could bring to bear – that is, *their* teaching methods and to educate him after *their* fashion. It was feared by some outsiders that such behaviour amounted to child abuse, and when Piran grew up, he would know nothing of Jock and Dai – he would be just another clone of George Senior and Mother; almost indistinguishable in fact from George Junior.

Another sibling of the family was Mick/Mike. Now, if Jock and Dai were 'problem children' and George Junior a 'spoilt brat', then Mick/Mike was an exceedingly difficult case. First of all, Mick/Mike had special needs – this is a euphemism; Mick/Mike was actually schizophrenic. You see, Mick believed he should live with his half brother, Paddy, on Europe Street. Paddy would look after him, thought Mick, and look after him much better than anyone else in his family. Yet at other times, the Mike personality was more dominant. Mike couldn't bear the idea of being cut loose from his Mother's apron strings. These inner tensions between Mick and Mike caused deep periods of sickness in the boy, but nobody seemed very concerned. It was only when Mick (*never* Mike) attacked George Senior or Mother physically, that people took any notice. And even then, after some angry words had been exchanged between George Senior and Mick (*never* Mike), there would be a lull again. But this lull was quite phoney – the boy often had violent debates with himself in the privacy of his own room. What was worse, Mick/Mike was self-harming.

Then we have George Junior's, Jock's, Dai's, Piran's and Mick/Mike's half brother, Paddy. Paddy had left the Britten household some years ago. He was now living by himself on Europe Street and was friendly with Francis/Frances Farr, Jerry Berlin, Diego Madrid and many others. In fact, Europe Street was a vibrant, multicultural street, and Paddy definitely felt more at home there than he had ever been in the Britten household. He had been undernourished whilst he was there – now, on Europe Street, he would no longer go hungry. When he had left initially, there had been fireworks, tears and recriminations on all sides – but Paddy was a determined fellow and he wanted to be free of the bickering inside the Britten family home. He didn't want to be associated with his dysfunctional family ever again, so when he left, he decided to change his name and henceforth called himself Paddy Ayre.

So, taking his future in his own hands, Paddy had stormed out, and eventually found a home for himself on Europe Street, where he was very happy. His neighbours would sometimes help him out and he would reciprocate – but he never felt that he had compromised his position of maintaining his own individuality. Working together and pooling resources with mutual respect on all sides, working towards a common, mutually beneficial goal was the aim and it was a breath of fresh air to Paddy after the strife of living in the Britten household. Paddy felt really happy on Europe Street.

A distant cousin of the family, Douglas Mann, lived independently of the Britten family, some two blocks away. He had nothing to do with Europe Street however, and tended to keep away from such places. However, he was not anti-social, and he often held parties for the well-to-do in his flat, all of whom assured their host that they were having a good time. Every year, Douglas would invite his friends to his country retreat where they could watch or take part in his motorcycling extravaganza.

Lez Ayre was one such good friend of Douglas's although she really liked only girls. She was very much into the leather scene surrounding the bikers too, along with her girlfriend, Ella N. Vannin. She was also distantly related to Paddy Ayre (né Britten).

Having touched upon some people having connections with the Britten household, often from a distance, such as Francis/Frances Farr, Jerry Berlin and Diego Madrid, we have yet to meet perhaps the most important individual in this town – and George Senior's boss – 'Uncle' Sam Washington.

'Uncle' Sam Washington was probably the most powerful man in town. He had interests in many pies and watched over the other citizens like a hawk. He was not averse to controlling their lives either and making them think how he thought and to buy (whether they could afford to or not) the things that he bought. If they did not agree with 'Uncle' Sam Washington's ideas, they were liable to be thrown out of the myriad properties that he owned and rented out to them in town and to be replaced by more acquiescent tenants. This was why George Senior and Mother made sure that they paid their rent regularly and on time to 'Uncle' Sam Washington. They also believed that because they did that, they had a 'special relationship' with 'Uncle' Sam Washington. For his part, 'Uncle' Sam Washington would give out little treats (essentially, sops to keep them quiet) to the Britten family and pay lip service to this 'special relationship' – and, as previously noted, he was George Senior's employer at YooKay Ltd, a wholly-owned 'Uncle' Sam Washington subsidiary company.

However, there was one area in particular where 'Uncle' Sam Washington could play on this 'special relationship' – if you will excuse the pun. It was a historical proven fact that one of 'Uncle' Sam Washington's forebears had actually left the Britten family house some time ago in the past. This action had fired up the imagination of Paddy Ayre (né Britten) in a later generation as we have seen, and also to a lesser extent, Jock and Dai. It was with this idea in mind that he had adopted the name of 'Uncle' – a word that conjured up images of fun, easy-goingness, generosity and yes, family. In tipping a wink to his ancestors, 'Uncle' Sam Washington maintained the goodwill of the Brittens (well, at least the older generation and probably, George Junior too) in a way probably unique in town. Sadly for Jock and Dai, he barely recognised them – often mistaking them for George Junior, or if corrected, he would ask,

"And who are you, again?"

I hope you liked my introduction to the Britten family and to their associates. I can only speak for myself – What a bunch!

19 Dear Catriona I ...

Hey girls! We're pleased to announce a new feature to your magazine of choice, *New Scotswoman Today*. An experienced and esteemed journalist, Catriona Alba has decided to write for us in the capacity of agony aunt. She has a long and proud history of resolving disputes and of empathising with her readers. We invite you therefore, ladies *and* gentlemen (no sexism here at *New Scotswoman Today*), to write in with *any* problems you may have, and Catriona will answer them for you. Here is a selection of what Catriona has already received.

The Editor, *New Scotswoman Today*

1 Dear Catriona,

I am suffering very badly at the hands of my husband in my marriage. He no longer respects me nor treats me as an equal partner and I am contemplating a divorce. Over the years I have suffered from domestic violence and other forms of abuse. He has always taken my money and then given me back just enough to get by on while he has gone on boozy foreign trips with his mates, in particular, Joe Washington. It has been a constant struggle to make ends meet. My husband has so much power over me that it is he who decides how and when we have sex. Now I'm a natural hot-blooded woman, but he fails to turn me on. When we *do* have sex – at his decision – it's all rather monotonous and predictable. I get very little satisfaction out of our coupling too. He tends to favour the same position each time.

I am writing to you then in despair, Catriona. I am highly tempted to find a lover who respects and loves me for myself, treats me as an equal and who can give me fantastic sex. Or should I just divorce my husband and live as an independent woman? Please advise.

Yours,

A. Scott (Mrs.)
(Alba)

***

2 Dear Catriona,

I am fearful of losing my job. I have been, I believe, a good employee to my boss, in trying to deliver his goods to as many people as I can. However, it seems that no matter how highly I praise his goods, the customers are not buying. When I tell my boss this, he says I should push the goods harder. He doesn't seem to listen to me either. So, I'm caught between a rock and a hard place – if I can't shift these goods soon, I'm sure my boss will blame me and sack me. And the people are not buying our produce. I really need your help, Catriona. Please help!

Ruth D.
(Glasgow)

***

3 Dear Catriona,

I will shortly be going through a divorce from my husband. I don't want it to be a messy one – but I'm not sure about him. I would like some advice on how I can ensure a clean break and ensure that I get my fair share of our joint assets. What do you advise?

Yours, aye,

Nicola S.
(Glasgow)

***

4 Dear Catriona,

Why do the best laid schemes o' mice an' men gang aft agley?

Roberta Burns
(Ayrshire)

***

5 Dear Catriona,

I used to be part of the committee that ran the events for the residents on our street, Union Street. This would include such fun things as street parties, and I think we did a good job of controlling these events.

Now, another committee has taken on the responsibilities of running these important events for the local residents. There are even rumours that they are going to remove the street parties from Union Street to some other place. In any case, I feel at a loose end. Our committee was the natural committee for running street parties and I am unsure of how to respond to the new committee's actions. My first reaction is naturally one of disappointment, but now I harbour resentment that the residents are still enjoying themselves, despite our committee having been replaced by the new grouping. It's almost as if they've forgotten about us!

I also find myself disagreeing with *everything* the new committee's chairman, Alex, has to say. Is this normal? And how do I get my committee back in running the street parties on Union Street?

In despair,

Johann L.
(Glasgow)

***

6 Dear Catriona,

I love my husband dearly, but he is always away on some project or other. I believe that he is fighting hard to retain some contracts for himself and his company and I am very proud of him for doing this.

He is however showing a greater amount of interest in spiders than ever before. Should I be worried by this?

Yours, For Scotland,

Roberta Le B.
(Bannockburn)

***

7 Dear Catriona,

My heart is broken – never to be mended again! I've lost my prince! He was bonny and he was my darling. My young cavalier, even!

Will ye no' come back again, my darling Charlie?

Yours (in floods of tears),

Flora McD.
(Skye)

***

8 Dear Catriona,

I used to be in politics but am now retired. I thought I would take up a relaxing hobby like ornithology (that's bird watching, to you, dear). As I was looking through my binoculars one day (trying to catch a glimpse of the elusive Lesser Spotted Kennedy bird), I happened to see something rather strange in the lake at the bottom of my garden. (Yes, I can afford my own private lake – these public-owned lochs are only for the common people.)

Anyway, what did I see, but a very large green monster. Now my natural political inclination is to invite the general public along to my garden and see this monster for themselves. And charge them for the privilege, of course! You can't be too careful when it's a question of money, as all us canny Scots know!

The problem is that I don't know if I can really believe my eyes and swear that I saw a monster. I mean, I remember telling old Caledonia, the butler, one day that I had seen fairies at the bottom of my garden too. And he completely disbelieved me! Such impudence! I should have dismissed him on the spot. As it turned out, he left my employ of his own accord, a few weeks later ...

So, Catriona, my wee lassie, do I risk another humiliation from the great unwashed who will come to my gardens and not see the monster and blame me or do I invite them, hope the monster makes an appearance and charge them entry to see it and make a quick profit? (Photographs of monster extra, of course).

Annabel G.
(Inverness)

20 Passenger announcement for those travelling by Scot Rail

"Good morning, ladies and gentlemen. My name is Alex and I am your chief guard on this train today. Welcome aboard this Scot Rail service to Independence, which is the end of the line and where this service will terminate. We will be calling at Essennpee, Ewing Central, Devolution Halt, Parliament and Independence. Expected time of arrival at Independence is around 20.14. However, please note that, owing to engineering work on the line, this could delay our journey. Additionally, work in replacing the track by outside contractors in the Devolution Halt area will mean that we will be shunted off the main track and find ourselves in the sidings for some time. Please bear with us, as we hope to be back on the main track before too long thereafter and making up for that lost time. We wish you a pleasant onward journey with us and we thank you for travelling with Scot Rail."

21 Farmer MacDonald

Old Farmer MacDonald had a farm, and on that farm he had a pair of wellington boots. They were a red, white and blue pair and they were well past their best. They were old and starting to split along their seams. They leaked water very badly, so that every time Farmer MacDonald strode around his farm he would as often as not return home with sodden feet. The wellies were often caked in mud and grime too, picked up by Farmer MacDonald as he went about his farm business. Additionally, his feet had started to swell in these wellies – or maybe the wellies themselves had got a little tighter; no one was too sure which. In any case, Farmer

MacDonald started to feel distinctly uncomfortable and to suffer some degree of pain when he wore the red, white and blue wellies.

Farmer MacDonald's wife had long ago given up on these wellies and it was her intention to throw them away at the earliest possible opportunity. His wife then was a highly practical woman. She also wanted the best for her husband and wanted him to appear smart in front of all the other farmers. So she bought some new wellies for her husband. These were bright and shiny and had, as yet, to be tried out on the farm. Farmer MacDonald loved his wife and always respected her decisions when it came to deciding things that were good for him. Indeed, being a far-sighted woman, his wife knew that what was good for Farmer MacDonald was not only good for her, but good for the farm as a whole. With these factors in mind, Farmer MacDonald got hold of the tatty, muck covered, painful old red, white and blue wellingtons and threw them into the rubbish bin. Then, with a smile and a wink to his wife, he slipped on the comfortable, new and shiny blue and white wellies and strode off to new pastures on his farm. His work was much more enjoyable as a result.

22 It's time!

There was once in a city, not so far away, a big, important antiques shop. This shop was initially run as a partnership by Mr Scott and Mr England. Now Mr Scott was the public face of the shop – it was he that would greet you from behind the counter – but you never got to see Mr England. It was said that Mr England managed the accounts and was more of a sleeping partner in the enterprise as opposed to Mr Scott who did all the daily, monotonous running of the shop. It was rumoured – but never fully proved – that in such a capacity, Mr England could 'cook the books' to his own advantage. Anyway, the unequal partnership of the antiques shop limped on, with Mr Scott having nary an angry word to say about his partner.

Now, pride of place in this antiques shop was an old clock. This old clock was valued by both partners of the antiques shop – and maybe more so by Mr England. Although superficially attractive, there was a problem: The clock did not go. It was this that probably prevented it from being sold to any of the antiques shop's customers. It had stopped in fact at a few minutes after 5pm, or to use the Continental fashion, 17.07. Now, whether due to laziness or inadequacy on the part of Mr England and Mr Scott, neither had been able to make this clock move forward. It was like it was caught in its own time warp – to be stuck forever at seven minutes past five.

Mr England and Mr Scott became old men and not able to fully perform their duties in the antiques shop. So they decided to lease out the premises to new tenants. First, there was Mr Dewar – but he didn't stay very long. Then came Mr McLeish, but his tenancy, too, was a very brief one. Mr McConnell followed, and he ran the antiques shop for almost six years. In all the time that these three tenants were running the antiques shop and were tenants of Mr England and Mr Scott, they too failed in setting the elegant clock to work. People came from far and wide to the antiques shop to see if the old clock was working, and, despite, many promises from these successive tenants that they would fix the clock's mechanism, they never really got round to it.

And then, a new, fresh-faced young tenant of the antiques shop materialised. Alex, for that was the young antiques dealer's name, decided that he wanted to be a new broom which swept clean through the old antiques shop. Mr England and Mr Scott were distrustful of young Alex, but knowing that they had to get money from somewhere, somewhat reluctantly agreed to his being their tenant. Alex immediately set to work and along with his girlfriend, Nicola and their friends, they cleaned up all the cobwebs that covered the shop's wares and brought in some well needed light so that its customers could see clearer the objects that were thinking of buying. The cabinet that Alex buffed up looked bright, shiny and polished after he had set his hand to it. Early on in his tenancy, Alex was constantly pestered by Mr Grey who wanted to buy the shop's lease from him, but on every occasion, Alex rebuffed him and continued his good work in the antiques shop.

Having by now settled down to running the antiques shop as a thriving business, Alex turned his attention to the old clock which had stopped at seven minutes past five. He knew that if he could get the clock going he could sell it and the antiques shop would make a healthy profit. Because of the huge successes that Alex had already achieved – thanks to his making the shop more airy and light, as previously mentioned and in attracting new and more customers to the shop than ever before – he was now working much later hours than any of his predecessors. He took out his watch from his waistcoat pocket and examined it. It was a little before quarter past eight in the evening, or 20.14. Alex smiled and said to himself,

"It's time!"

Alex studied the old stopped clock's mechanism again. He knew what was missing: Jenkins's Scottish spring™. Those former tenants and wind up merchants had obviously overlooked something. Alex applied the all-important piece of equipment. And lo! For the first time in many years that clock ticked and moved forward. Alex set it at the correct time and smiled again. The clock told the proper time for the first time for ages. It was a historic moment and Alex would savour it. Alex was thrilled – and he knew the antiques shop's customers would be too.

23 Tannoy announcement

"Welcome to Scotland Central railway station. On Platform 1, there is the rickety, clapped out 17.07 service to Nowhere. This service calls at Nowhere only. We apologise to passengers for the late running of this train owing to the fact that it has broken down many times already and needs to be equipped with rear view mirrors. This train will also be travelling backwards with regard to the driver. That's Platform 1, for the 17.07 service to Nowhere.

On Platform 2 there is the 20.14 express service to Independence, calling at Feel Good, Higher Prosperity, Happiness and Independence. That's the

20.14 express service to Independence, on Platform 2.

Platform number 3 for the Ermine Gravy Train due to leave at 20.16. This train is for Lords House and calls at Unionist Central, Conlabdem and Lords House. Passengers wishing to go to Europa, please change at Conlabdem. That's the 20.16 Ermine Gravy Train for Lords House."

24 The wine connoisseurs

There were once two wine connoisseurs who liked to debate about their knowledge of wine. They would sometimes resort to metaphor and parable in order to try and get their message across. This use of allegory was often used by them in other fields too, such as politics and history. They tended to think they were very erudite and in consequence, rather superior to the usual *hoi polloi*.

"Let us take the Union between England and Scotland," said the first wine connoisseur one day. "It seems to me that this is like a great champagne.

It is the classiest of drinks and blends sweetness with mellifluous bubbles, the perfect mixture. It sparkles on every occasion it is brought out. It is appreciated worldwide as the peak in wine producing. And it is very refreshing on the palate."

"I agree that the relationship between Scotland and England can be compared to wine," said the second man, "but champagne is the wrong example. You say it sparkles on every occasion, but this wine goes flat very quickly and is only appreciated by the well to do who can afford to quaff it. Further, it promises so much, but turns out to be, for the most part, mere froth. It has no body. A fine *vin de table* is more readily appreciated, and by more people, north and south of the border – a wine that retains its own individual character, be it white or red, and is cultivated by the people who drink it in their own vineyards. It is a much more inclusive drink than champagne. Importantly too, for those canny, thrifty Scots, it does not hit the pocket as hard as champagne either."

I'm afraid that we'll have to leave our two wine experts agreeing to disagree.

But which wine will tickle your taste buds in September 2014?

25 The sun and the snowflake

"Ha!" said the sun one day. "How weak and insignificant you are, little snowflake! Why, I could melt you with one wink of my eye."

"Perhaps," replied the little snowflake. "But you'll find it much harder to get rid of us when thousands and thousands of us cover the land."

The sun set an angry red colour.

26 That's charming, darling!

"My name is Alistair, darling," said the old smoothie to Ms. Alba at the party. "I want you to say 'No.' That's what turns me on."

Don't we girls prefer to be seduced, asked what *we* like (and not be told by the man what *he* likes) and then say "YES"?

27 The chimpanzees

The chimpanzees in the rain forest that covered the island of Cambria were a happy bunch. They could swing through the trees at will, chatter to each other in their own vernacular and they had a rich supply of bananas. The trees of the rain forest also protected them from the fiercest of storms and their lives were generally ones of pleasant ease and communal co-operation.

Then one day, an event shook the chimpanzee population of the island of Cambria as never before. Tall, strong, multi-talented two-legged animals moved onto the island. They started to burn down the rain forest. The chimpanzees fled inland, to less favourable living conditions, shouting wildly at their fellows that their old way of life was being destroyed. But this did not disturb the new arrivals – on the contrary, they began shooting the chimpanzees out of hand, killing and wounding scores in the process. Those that they did not kill, the two legged animals seized as trophies and took back to their ships offshore.

"No more monkey business here" joked one of these two-legged, gun wielding animals.

"True" said another one, guffawing loudly. "Only that monkeys will be *our* business." He laughed again, a deep, raucous laugh that further upset the surviving chimpanzees.

The dead chimpanzees were thrown unceremoniously into the sea off Cambria island. The two-legged animals then threw the wounded ones onto their ships and sailed away – but not before torching the chimpanzees' homes. Some poked fun at the chimpanzees, others placed large wooden planks around their necks – a symbol of their servility and barbarity in not speaking like the two-legged animals (who, it must be said, were actually distant cousins of the chimpanzees.) The chimpanzees then would be routinely thrashed – and forced to wear the two-legged animals' clothes, to give some semblance of what the two-legged animals, considered to be the epitome of good grace, civilisation and breeding. As a reward, the chimpanzees would often receive peanuts – and they had to be grateful for those. The free, sweet bananas of Cambria were but a faded memory to the chimpanzees.

But there were still some chimpanzees who kept alive the ideas of their homeland and the freedom that they had enjoyed on the island of Cambria before being enslaved and ridiculed by the two-legged animals, before they had burnt down their dwellings and killed so many of their fellow chimpanzees. Would the surviving chimpanzees be strong and numerous enough to instigate a revolution and turn back the two-legged animals who had destroyed their habitats, mocked their barbaric chattering and decimated their population? Time would surely tell.

28 The two cars

"Roll up, punters, to the greatest car sale show that Scotland has ever had! Or at least the biggest car show in over three hundred years. We have two prime exhibits for you today and we are letting you decide which motor you'd like to take home with you.

First up is this vintage, red, white and blue little number which is being offered for sale by Darling and Associates. I'm afraid that despite having many miles on the clock it has very little to commend it as a practical modern vehicle. Its engine has been known to seize up on many occasions, resulting in breakdowns and lengthy and costly visits to garages. Any repairs effected have at best appeared to be cosmetic, as the whole crate breaks down regularly. The steering is a bit suspect – sometimes it veers to the left, at other times it swerves to the right, and this despite the best ingenuity of the driver. It's almost as if this vehicle has a will of its own and will take the driver and its occupants to any place but where the motorist wishes to go. Being a vintage model of course means that it has had many, many previous owners. This will explain the ripped upholstery, the mud patches inside the car, and the various dents to the body where the vehicle has not come off best in the various scrapes it has endured with other road users.

Knowing that Scots are careful with money, I can honestly tell you that this vehicle is not very economically effective – it is in fact, a guzzler of fuel (usurped from the North Sea) and pays little attention to the effect such consumption has on the environment. It is my guess, ladies and gentlemen of Scotland, that being reasonable people, and considering the pedigree of the company offering you this vehicle, you will refuse to be sold it. For let's be clear – this is not do much a car that breaks down, is unenvironmentally friendly, uses up your hard-earned money by burning your oil and petrol with ease, not going the way you wish to steer it, but rather a pup. And Darling and Associates are doing you a great disservice, I believe the Managing Director went to the Boyce School for Car Salesmen in Peckham, London, in attempting to flog you this piece of worthless junk.

Our second model, by contrast is a gleaming, shiny, new blue and white vehicle – top of the range. Offered to you today by the Y.E.S. Scotland garage, I cannot recommend this vehicle too highly to you. It is, I dare suggest, the vehicle of choice for all right thinking Scotsmen and Scotswomen. Despite its colour, it is in fact a 'green' car. (Ha ha!). Run on home-produced convertibles, it is far more economic to run and will take you from here to wherever you want to go – no dodgy steering here! Its very newness counts in its favour and is guaranteed to turn the heads of your neighbours. And you want technology? All the latest technology for both safe navigation and car safety as well as and entertainment via USB slots and radio come as standard in this vehicle.

I think the options are very clear – as is the decision about which car you will buy, dear ladies and gentlemen of Scotland. Insist on the best vehicle in the show – and you'll be going places!"

29 Angus Alba and his shirts

Angus Alba was what you might call a typical man. Rugged yet handsome, one of the lads but also fairly intelligent and politically aware, he was considered to be a good catch – that is if any of the lassies of the village could catch him. However, not only would she have to fight off the other lassies to ensure that she became Angus's 'one'; she would also have to deal with one of Angus's less appealing traits – one which made him perhaps even more 'blokey', but decidedly less appealing to members of the fairer sex.

Angus was notorious in the village for his red, white and blue striped shirt. This in itself caused much blethering to circulate about him; usually negative in character. However, and what repelled others was that this shirt was in a distinct state of disrepair and generally in a filthy, dirty condition. The shirt had obviously seen better days; now it was badly torn in many areas, and the remains of various repasts in the Alba household had left multi-coloured stains of their own on the shirt. There were those who said that Angus slept in the same shirt he wore of a daytime. This fact, although never actually proved, was all the more readily believed by the villagers, as it never seemed to have seen the face of a flat iron.

Be that as it may, one strapping, independent-minded lass in the village, Nicola, by name, decided to tackle the matter head on and to make Angus her beau too. Nicola was a feisty character and she was up to the challenge that faced her. She also knew that Angus dallied occasionally with Johann. This latter character's reputation for 'likin' a wee bit o' ruff' had it seemed made her favourite to win Angus's permanent affections. But Nicola was a determined young lady; 'thrawn' the locals described her to be. She knew that if she could turn Angus to her way of thinking, that ultimately the whole village would be pleased that Angus had bettered himself. More importantly, Angus would begin to appreciate his own worth too.

Nicola confronted the matter straight on. The red, white and blue shirt would have to go. No matter how attached Angus was to that shirt, it was clearly beyond repair and Nicola would not stand for it polluting the atmosphere of her house if she was going to stay with Angus. Further, the shirt did no service to Angus himself. Did he not realise that the rest of the village would often hold their noses as he went past wearing that garment? Angus's image was as torn as the shirt itself – 'aye, it was lookin' michtie scoorie' – it did little to keep him warm and obviously he did not look in the least bit smart in it.

Angus pleaded with Nicola. He begged her that he should keep the shirt. The shirt was as much of his body as his limbs were by now. He had grown attached to the shirt in the same way that many men do to otherwise obsolete and worn out clothes. It was part of who he was – Angus and the red, white and blue striped shirt, that was him. And he was known in the village for having that shirt. He and the shirt had some sort of male bonding or loyalty to each other. In any case, what right had she, Nicola, to tell him what was what? He'd worn that shirt for years before she had come along and he would do so again. He said that Nicola was 'yammering' at him and treating him like a child.

Nicola persisted. Yes, Angus was known in the village for wearing that shirt. But that was the point. Nicola told him in no uncertain terms that, 'She was'nae fessin' o'er nothing.' It was only for wearing that dreadful, tatty, filthy shirt that he was known. Did he not want to better himself and look elegant and be admired by his fellow villagers instead of looking like something that had been dragged though a hedge backwards? Yes, Nicola was yammering at him. But she believed that he could do better, so much better if he didn't wear that shirt.

The arguments raged. And then Nicola had an idea. She put the red, white and blue shirt on herself. She mushed her hair, took off her earrings and started to slouch in front of Angus, in much the same way that he would mooch about the village. Angus was appalled. For despite her 'yammering', he had started to feel a grudging feeling of respect; maybe not love, at least not yet, for Nicola for sticking to her guns in trying to better him. Perhaps there was something in what she said after all? Angus stared at the woman in the red, white and blue tatty shirt in front of him and rubbed his eyes.

"Yae luik affa, lassie," was all that Angus could say.

"Aye ye're michtie richt there," replied Nicola. "An' that's hou you luik fan yae skulk aboot the village in this damn shirt."

"Oh wad some pow'r the giftie gi'e us, to see

ourselves as others see us," sighed Angus, remembering some poetry he had learned at school years ago.

"Aye, my cannie laddie" said Nicola softly. "Tha's it fairly spoken. Thon's whit folks in the village see to yersell. And now yae can see yersell in me – as in a glass."

Angus was silent for a long time. Finally, he said:

"Whit shall I dae, Nicola?"

"First things first: We bin this useless aul red, white and blue shirt, richt?"

Angus nodded silently.

"Then," Nicola went on in a businesslike manner, "you'll be wearing this bonnie new shirt I've bought fer yae."

And removing the old shirt, Nicola put on a bright blue and white shirt which she had bought the other day at Salmonds the tailors. Angus was impressed.

"Thon's an affa stotter o' a shirt, lassie," he whistled softly.

"Nought but the best to be found at Salmonds," said Nicola, giving a wink.

"You luik affa, affa bonnie yersel lass," went on Angus.

"Weel ... try it on then yae big lummox," said Nicola.

Angus seized the shirt and marched into the house. When Nicola followed him inside, there was Angus preening himself like a peacock in front of the glass.

"It's me!" he kept shouting. "It's the real me!"

"Aye it is that," smiled Nicola. "Now Angus, yer a fair secht fer sair eyes! And I would'nae want anything less than the best for my future husband."

Angus could hardly refuse; Nicola had done all this for him. He would soon realise that the villagers would have a new respect for him now: clean, tidy, elegant and with a good, practical, no-nonsense wife. And in the best traditions of these romances, they both lived happily ever after.

Coda

Johann, when she realised that she had lost Angus forever, left the village, crossed the river, moved south and lived the rest of her days on a council estate. She made new friends, among them Dave, Nick, Alastair, Ruth, Ed and Charlie. This last one however was rarely seen by the other inhabitants on the estate and it was thought that he must have been doing some high-level governmental hush-hush work. But this was never proven.

30 How about some wine, Scotland?

We cast our eyes over two highly-competitive wines in our local supermarket, so that we can help you choose the perfect accompaniment to your food. Write in and tell us which one you will vote for.

The Editor, *Scottish Wines Today* magazine

<u>Château Darling 2012</u>

A sharp, rather acidic and dry white. Rather unpalatable to most tastes and cold. Does not travel well when exported from southern realms to more northerly climes. Best kept in a deep, dark cellar. When it comes to wines, this is more like a *whine* than a *wine*. This is a wine for laying down and avoiding. A wine which will disagree with you, and you with it. The only point in common being that it has a taste which wants you to say "NO" – and you will agree: No more of this horrible beverage. If this wine leaves you with a bad aftertaste in the mouth, (which is more likely than not), apply Salmond's™ patent mouthwash, rinsing mouth thoroughly. In serious cases, a visit to Neil's General Hospital may be necessary. All in all, probably not a wine to your taste.

Jenkins's Champagne 2014

A sweet sparkling and cheerful wine, made from our best grapes from our Elgin vineyard. Has matured over the years at both Château STV and BBC du Pape. In our humble opinion, the wine of choice for the majority of Scottish oenophiles. To be consumed in *immoderation*, in particular, when celebrating notable national victories. Best served with a lot of 'Ayes' (ice).

31 *Gwrthryfel!*

Pentref bach ar lan y môr ydy Aberllanw. Mae'n bentref bach hyfryd, yn llawn bwrlwm, a'r Gymraeg yw'r unig iaith a glywch ar ei strydoedd ac yn y siopau. Mae pawb yn adnabod ei gilydd a phawb yn barod eu cymwynas. Mae Aberllanw yn manteisio hefyd o'i leoliad – môr a thraeth godidog i'r de a mynyddoedd gwyrdd, hardd i'r gogledd. A dweud y gwir, i unrhyw Gymro neu Gymraes, mae Aberllanw yn rhyw baradwys fach, ac yn rhywle lle gallwch ymlacio ac anghofio am bryderon y byd a rhai chi'ch hun.

Dewch draw felly, i'r tŷ tafarn lleol – y Llew Du. Cewch groeso brwdfrydig yno bob tro, peint neu ddau, cwmpeini difyr ac yn bennaf oll, bwyd da cartref wedi ei goginio gan y chef, *Rhys. Brawd Rhys, Gethin sy'n rhedeg y Llew Du gyda'i wraig, Eileen, a hi yw'r barmêd. Ond seren y dafarn ydy Rhys, a chydnabyddir ei ddawn fel* chef *trwy'r holl fro.*

Fodd bynnag, mae i Rys ddawn arall sy'n cael ei chydnabod yn Aberllanw. Y mae, er gwell, er gwaeth, yn dipyn o benboethyn ac yn genedlaetholwr. Er bod trigolion Aberllanw yn ymhyfrydu yn eu Cymreictod, yn arddel yr iaith yn eu bywydau beunyddiol, nid yw'n fater politicaidd iddynt hwy. Mae Rhys yn ddigon hir ei ben i weld y don o Seisnigrwydd sy'n boddi nifer o gymunedau Cymraeg a Chymreig mewn rhannau eraill o Gymru, ac yn gweld na fydd yn hir cyn i Aberllanw hefyd gael ei sgubo i mewn i'r lli hwnnw. Ond i weddill trigolion Aberllanw, does dim problem – maen nhw'n parhau i sgwrsio yn "yr hen iaith," a fydd yna ddim newid yn Aberllanw.

Ac yna, mae *pethau'n dechrau newid. Mae ail-*

strwythuro yn rheolaeth y bragdy cenedlaethol Seisnig sydd biau'r Llew Du yn dod â chymeriad newydd i mewn i'r stori – Mr Grey o Ruthun. Sais uniaith yw Mr Grey ac mae'n dechrau ar ei swydd fel uwch-reolwr Gethin yn y pentref. Mae angen "moderneiddio'r" dafarn a denu mwy o bobl o'r tu allan. Ac yn hyn o beth, mae angen "moderneiddio'r" pentref hefyd. Ni fydd yn caniatau i neb siarad Cymraeg yn y Llew Du mwyach – boed yn staff neu'n gwsmer. Mae'n ffyrnigo wrth glywed Mrs Beasley, y bostfeistres, yn siarad â chwsmer yn "that silly language" *ac yn honni eu bod yn siarad amdano ef. Mae cysgod y* "Welsh Not" *dros Aberllanw.*

Un diwrnod, mae Rhys, Gethin ac Eileen yn cael hoe fach wrth y bar yn y Llew Du yn trafod pethau â'i gilydd yn Gymraeg. Mae Mr Grey yn cerdded i mewn ac yn syth mae'n clywed yr iaith na ddeallai yn cael ei siarad. Mae'n gwylltio'n gacwn ac yn mynnu eu bod yn siarad yn Saesneg yn ei ŵydd ef. Mae hyn yn ffyrnigo Rhys yntau – neu "Reece" *fel mae ei gyflogwr yn ei alw. Ymddiswyddodd Rhys yn y fan a'r lle, ac mae'n rhuthro allan o'r dafarn. Fel arwydd o gefnogaeth, mae Gethin ac Eileen hwythau yn ymddiswyddo, gan addo dialedd ar Mr Grey.*

Mae pethau yn awr yn symud yn eu blaenau'n gyflym, gyda phethau'n troi o gwmpas y penboethyn o chef, *Rhys. Ys dywed un o drigolion y pentref,*

"Mae'r Llanw'n troi."

Y catalydd a symbylydd y 'troi' hwn yw Rhys, sydd bellach i'w weld fel "merthyr" i'r achos. Fodd bynnag, nid yw ef ei hun yn gweld mai safbwynt ferthyraidd yw'r un i'w mabwysiadu; i'r gwrthwyneb, mae Rhys eisiau byw er mwyn talu'r pwyth yn ôl i Mr Grey. Mae Rhys yn cysylltu â'i gyfreithiwr, Owain, ac mae hwnnw bellach yn cael ei weld fel arweinydd gwrthryfel trigolion Aberllanw yn erbyn eu gormeswr o Sais, Mr Grey. Daw Owain ag achos llys o ddiswyddo anghyfiawn yn erbyn Mr Grey, ar ran ei gleientiaid, Rhys, Gethin ac Eileen. Ond mae ganddo gyfreithiwr cyfrwys a galluog ar yr ochr arall i'w drechu'n gyntaf – Henry Forth. Ac mae Henry Forth o'r un dras â'i gleient yntau, Mr Grey.

Mae'r frwydr am fod yn un anodd i Gymry Aberllanw.

32 John

John's early life had been quite eventful up to the age of nine, and looking back on it, he considered the blessings he had derived from and disadvantages that he had suffered during that time – not least because of his aptitude for languages and the constant reminder of his 'burden of nationality.'

John was born into a bilingual English-French family in Sussex; considered by many to be the heart of English speaking England. His parents were mother tongue English speakers, but owing to the fact that both of them had spent many years previously working in France, they had also picked up a considerable amount of French too.

When John was around 3 years old both his parents lost their jobs in England. They decided then as a family that a new venture could be made for themselves in France. John's mother and father reckoned they could very easily adapt themselves to the local conditions and that John himself, once he entered the local *école primaire* would become as bilingual as they were.

At that time, there was a shortage of workers who could tend the local vineyard in Saint-Marc-l'Eglise, a little village in the heart of the south eastern French countryside. John's parents applied for jobs, and were much surprised to learn by return of post that their candidatures had been accepted.

Once the necessary employment paperwork had been filled in, the family were found accommodation by the vineyard owner and they settled down. John, at that time a monoglot English speaker, was then sent to the *école primaire*, and everyone seemed to be very happy. His parents decided that his mother would speak to him only in French, whilst to maintain his English, John's father would converse with the boy only in that language. It was doubly advantageous that in his spare time, the male adult also composed children's stories in English which he would present to his son in both manuscript and cassette tape format; thus enabling the boy to keep his mother tongue and strengthen both his reading and listening skills in that language.

Now it must be imagined that Saint-Marc-l'Eglise was a small, rural commune – one so indicative of the French countryside. A few houses, the church, the school, everyone knowing everyone else, quiet and tranquil, with a population of barely 300 and obviously, thoroughly and completely French speaking, that was Saint-Marc-l'Eglise. It was into this society that John's family – *les anglais* – had come and they were soon to find out that not everyone was welcoming.

As is often the case, it is the weakest of a grouping

which can be identified first. In this case, it was John. First of all, it was very subtle. John and his family were strict vegetarians. To a rural community used to farms and livestock this behaviour was at best, strange; at worst, highly irregular and marked off a distinction immediately between the in-comers and the local population. To accommodate the problem, a simple application of uniformity and harmonisation was applied – John would have meat in his school dinner like the rest of the children, or he could go hungry until going home time. Being a mere pawn in this process and not wishing to appear awkward to his hosts, John swallowed both his pride and his carnivorous repasts.

It also soon became apparent, not least because of the influences of languages and literature back home that John was destined to became a thorough and balanced English-French bilingual. There is also the scientifically proven fact that youngsters at a very early age take in, sponge like, information, facts and yes, language very early on, with seemingly no trouble at all. They are naturally curious in any case and will soak up these things and become mini-walking and talking encyclopaedias in no time. It will be borne in mind that all education at the *école primaire* in Saint-Marc-l'Eglise was through the medium of French – no concession was made to John in that he knew no French at all prior to entry. And he was never to be taught anything through the medium of English either, of course. All of his classmates were already native speakers of French, and were thereby considered (and indeed considered themselves, in the normal, French *chauvin* fashion) to be more advantaged and superior to John.

What they were soon to find out – and it came as an unpleasant shock to them all – was that John's French soon outstripped theirs. The insults towards *les rosbifs* – such name calling being highly ironic, considering their initial vegetarianism – escalated; the bullying became more severe. One young French boy spoke with delight of his plan to throw a rotten tomato at John's father's face and crowed to his friends that he was just waiting his chance to effect it. (As it turned out, this threat was never put into action, as John's family were to move on a couple of years later.)

The most shocking behaviour however may be considered the attitude of *Madame l'Institutrice* of the *école primaire* at Saint-Marc-l'Eglise. Not only was she unable (or unwilling) to discipline her charges for their behaviour towards *le petit étranger*, but she decided on a new approach to her syllabus. It was evident that the native *camarades de classe* were falling behind in the development of their mother tongue – or maybe they were going at the usual pace of learning as any other native speaker – whilst John, *l'immigré, le petit anglais*, was streaking ahead. There had to be a way to stop him, and ensure that the others in the class did not lose their in-built French advantage – national and linguistic pride were at stake, and she, *Madame l'Institutrice* had the power to defend the integrity of both the French language and the French nation.

She then hit upon the following plan: John would be shunted off to a classroom by himself where he was permitted colouring pencils and a sheet of blank paper. He was then given a picture of a yacht sailing into a scarlet sunset and was ordered to reproduce this on his blank piece of paper. If he had not completed this exercise by the end of the day, he was to take it home and complete it there. In the meantime, John's monoglot French *camarades de classe* would receive further and remedial education in their native language, until they reached John's level of proficiency *in their own language*. This procedure continued for some months, with John returning his completed copy of the picture on a daily basis.

John's parents felt completely impotent in their new environment – they were *les nouveaux-venus* and all the cards seemed to be stacked in the school's and *Madame l'Institutrice*'s favour. There seemed little hope in appealing to the *Préfet* or the *Réctorat*: they would surely side with their compatriots against *les rosbifs* and *l'ennemi héréditaire*, in any case. John and his family would just have to stick it out.

And indeed, that is what they did, for the next two years or so – until a more lucrative job offer to John's family took them to another village in the south east of France and John to a different *école primaire*.

The constant identifier of being *l'étranger* would never leave John and he would be marked by these experiences from his formative years. His final grandparent – his father's mother – passed away when he was almost nine years old, and the family returned home to England in the expectation of being received back into their own community and acknowledged as being finally 'at home.' Events in the future years would prove how mistaken a belief this was too ...

33 The bee's knees is the business

Once upon a time, there was a big apiary in a field. The apiary was owned by a widow, Bea Keeper and her daughter, Melissa. Although they owned the apiary, the day to day running of it had been delegated by them to the bees themselves. In such a way, the apiary was a loose federal structure of hives, with a supreme queen bee in the most senior hive at its head. Below the senior hive were the other hives which would often co-operate with each other in the production of honey and in sharing resources.

The main resources of each hive were of course the

worker bees. These would go out on daily missions in order to search out new flowers and collect nectar in order to make honey. Invaluable in this procedure were the instructor bees of each hive; these could inform their fellow bees where the best flowers were to be had. Some of these instructor bees taught their colleagues through the medium of an elaborate dance technique. Others communicated the presence of flowers to other members of the hive by buzzing.

In order to achieve maximum efficiency in communication in the hives, the supreme queen bee had issued an edict that the whole apiary would treat the methods of instruction, dancing and buzzing, as being equal with each other in all respects, and that *any* hive would welcome any instructor bee having the appropriate skill in either dancing or buzzing. The benefits of worker bees knowing both dancing *and* buzzing were considered to be well-known and advantageous to both the individual hive and the apiary at large. In this edict, the supreme queen was also putting into effect what she knew that Bea Keeper and Melissa also wanted for their colony of bees.

Now, as previously mentioned, in order to fully maximise the potential of the apiary, there was a considerable amount of personal freedom between hive and hive. The bees often flew from one to another, making new friends and acquaintances as they did so, and learning new techniques and sharing stories.

One day, a vacancy for a dancing instructor bee appeared in one of the hives; a hive hitherto only known for having had buzzing instructor bees. A dancing instructor bee, called Mel, from another hive got to hear about it, and, considering both his aptitude and desire to change hives, he decided he would make an application for the post. Mel's own speciality was indeed instructing other bees in the dance technique; he even made a living out of it, and thereby avoided having to do any tiring flying himself. Additionally, he was also qualified in buzzing.

With the above factors in mind then, Mel made his application to the hive where the vacancy had arisen. In keeping to the spirit of the supreme queen's edict, and indeed both the nature of the post on offer, and his own speciality, he submitted a video of himself dancing. (It will be recalled that the supreme queen's edict treated prospective dancing instructor bees equally with prospective buzzing instructor bees.)

Mel then was rather surprised when he received a reply from the employing hive that the video was incompatible with their systems. A drone from that hive furthermore insisted that a fresh video – one of Mel buzzing – was required. This was indeed a rude surprise to Mel: the supreme queen's edict was being circumvented, and the applicant bee himself was being thwarted from presenting his case as a qualified dancing instructor not only through his own preferred means of communication, but also that which the hive wanted him to instruct them in, in the first place!

Mel, rather annoyed that he had been told to buzz off by the drone; one could say he had a bee in his bonnet now about the whole business, made a beeline for the supreme queen's hive, where he sought an audience with Her Majesty. He was given a very sympathetic hearing by her, and she promised to take the matter up on Mel's behalf.

The very next day, the supreme queen gave a buzz to the queen of the employing hive. She was fairly buzzing with rage at the indignity suffered by her subject, Mel. Furthermore, her own edict, regarding the equality of treatment between applicant dancing instructor bees and applicant buzzing instructor bees had clearly been breached. She was minded to tell Bea Keeper herself, and force her hand into smoking the employing hive and making the inferior queen of that hive toe the line.

It was a perfectly clear established principle of the apiary, that in cases where an incompatible video in a lower ranked hive could not be read, then it was for *that* hive to arrange for it to be sent to the supreme queen's hive for conversion, whereupon it would then be returned to the employing hive. It was *not* for an applicant instructor bee to either attempt his own conversion, or to resubmit another video in the format requested by the employing hive – both of which would have involved considerable time and expense by the applicant and may well not have been able to be submitted before the deadline imposed by the employing hive.

The queen of the employing hive was quiet for some time, and then realising that her silence might be interpreted as her condoning her drone's actions and that she was disobeying the supreme queen, she became very contrite. She apologised profusely to the supreme queen and asked for her apologies to be transmitted to Mel. She also apologised on behalf of her whole hive and the drone who had told Mel to make a fresh application. The initial video would be considered – in its converted form – by her personally and she would treat both Mel and any subsequent applicant dancing instructor bees equally with any buzzing instructor bees. She spoke for the whole hive when she said that they did not wish to be smoked out by Bea Keeper, and in future they would toe the supreme queen's line. In a nutshell, they would all bee hive ...

Mel himself danced with joy. He demonstrated both his dancing *and* buzzing talents at the subsequent job interview and became a highly successful and respected dancing instructor in his new hive.

That was the *real* sting in the tail!

34 Of mice and ... ?

There was once a nest of mice that lived quite contentedly together in the hole of a skirting board in the kitchen of an old house. Their diet was fairly ordinary, in that they mainly ate Caerphilly cheese. Some of the mice were known as educator mice, and their primary role was to instruct the rest of the nest on the merits of Caerphilly cheese. The mice had heard tell of more exotic cheeses like Dutch Edam and Danish Blue and some had even ventured far away from home in order to taste them – but these were rare creatures. Whilst undoubtedly these other good cheeses existed beyond the nest, it was often a perilous journey for any mouse to search them out, and the mouse population were often warned of dangers that lurked outside the nest. It was far better to stay within the comfort of the nest and continue with the diet of Caerphilly cheese, safe and secure in the knowledge that roaming further afield to sample those other exotic cheeses was fraught with dangers; travelling across open country to sample a Gorgonzola or an Emmental was tempting Providence and would as likely as not result in the death of any mouse venturing outside its home territory.

However, and as befits any community, this nest of mice had its share of what could be termed eccentrics. One such mouse, Lyn Gwist by name, was one such singular character. He had been a conscientious student at school and had learnt much about the other cheeses that lay beyond his nest of Caerphilly-eating compatriots. He found it rather hypocritical that he and his classmates had been told of such exotica as Cambozola and Gouda yet they had never sampled either. True, both of Lyn's parents had been brave (or was it foolhardy?) enough to risk trying out some Gruyère once, and had lived to tell the tale. But, in reality, Lyn's parents too were exceptional – the vast majority of the mice had lived on Caerphilly cheese for generations and were not to have their eating habits changed by a family of mavericks, something that undoubtedly Lyn and his family were.

Now in keeping with his family's mindset, Lyn himself could not bear the idea of being shackled to the monotonous and boring Caerphillian diet. Inheriting his family's wanderlust, he too wanted 'to see the world' and see what was on offer outside the nest. It was then that Lyn got wind of a large Camembert cheese being consumed by another nest of mice that lived in the facing skirting board of the kitchen. Lyn was sure he would like soft cheese, and coupled with his sense of adventure, he knew this was an opportunity not to be missed. Lyn's parents gave him all encouragement, only warning him to take care not to fall into traps, be wary of the house cat and not to eat anything suspicious on the way. They were also proud that their son was now making big decisions for himself.

As it was, Lyn's journey across the kitchen floor to the Camembert was quite uneventful. When he finally got to his destination Lyn saw that many mice from the other nest – and indeed, others who had travelled from far and wide to the Camembert-hosting nest — were already enjoying the feast or busy chatting to each other. Lyn was not a shy mouse by inclination and he soon began to talk to and exchange ideas with the other mice.

"My nest eats Caerphilly cheese," said Lyn proudly.

"What's that?" asked one of the other mice.

It was clear from the puzzled looks on many of the other mice's faces that they had no idea what this 'Caerphilly cheese' was. Lyn realised, and often through no fault of the other mice, they had no idea what his nest's speciality was – although Lyn himself was sufficiently knowledgeable of their

Mascarpones, Edams and Roqueforts. He saw that he would have to educate his new friends as to the merits of Caerphilly. He gave them a brief description of that cheese, and seeing that they appreciated what he was saying, he made a vow with them that he would return the following night with a sample of Caerphilly for them to taste.

Lyn returned home early the next morning, jubilant. Not only had he tasted that delicious Camembert, made some new friends, but he had also managed to enlighten those friends of the existence of his own nest and their predilection for Caerphilly cheese – another exotic (and to them, a previously unknown) cheese for them to sample. In consequence, Lyn, as promised, returned to the other nest regularly with batches of Caerphilly for his new friends, and when they were not feasting on it they were chatting to each other and professing how exceedingly good the Caerphilly was and how it complemented and indeed, supplemented the Camembert.

One could imagine that Lyn was in his element and

exceedingly happy. And one would be right – but only up to a point. Lyn's nightly trips across the kitchen floor were still fraught with danger; what with the ever-present threat of the cat, the poison and the traps and of course the effort in carrying the Caerphilly by himself to his new friends. They were perhaps not confident enough in themselves to traverse the kitchen floor to Lyn's nest or, more likely, they were more than happy for Lyn to do all the work himself. And Lyn did not fail them as he shuttled back and forth nightly between his own nest and the nest which hosted the Camembert.

Lyn, by now established as the 'big cheese in supplying Caerphilly' began to extol to his home nest the advantages that were accruing to that nest from his work among his new friends on the other side of the kitchen. Caerphilly cheese was finally being recognised outside their own nest and those mice who had not tasted it before were singing its praises. Furthermore, the other mice were previously unaware that they shared the kitchen with Lyn's nest – but out of respect to him they would not fight with the other mice for territorial rights; on the contrary, Lyn was an excellent ambassador, they were all mice when it came down to it, and they had the same enemies. Far better to work together for the common good of all mice everywhere: The Mice of the World, The World of Mice.

Lyn now decided to up his nest's profile. He visited the educator mice of his nest, he had conversations with the suppliers of Caerphilly cheese, he spoke to his fellow mice, he wrote articles about his experiences in the nest's journals. He even corresponded with the Chief Mouse of the nest. Lyn suggested to all his fellow mice that it would be a really good idea if his professional standing amongst the mice across the kitchen floor were maintained, and more importantly, the good name of his home nest, if another member of the Caerphilly eating mice were to join him. Wouldn't that raise their profile even further? Wouldn't the Caerphilly be easier to carry between a team of dedicated, committed mice, as opposed to Lyn having to do it all by himself? Furthermore, Lyn had to pay the suppliers in the first place out of his own pocket for the Caerphilly which he ferried across the kitchen floor – a journey, which if taken with others would also minimise the risks of danger too. It was also quite costly for him to do it all by himself.

Lyn's appeals for support – both moral and financial – were given short shrift by the nest's leaders. The Chief Mouse commended his efforts, but those fine words buttered no parsnips for Lyn. The educator mice (it will be remembered that they were those responsible for pushing the Caerphilly diet on the other mice) also offered platitudes, or in some extreme cases, complete negativity towards Lyn's proposals. Ordinary nest mice either shrugged their shoulders and returned to their Caerphilly or pointed out that they did not have the resources to acquire the Caerphilly themselves from the suppliers (the erroneous assumption being that

Lyn was wealthy enough to do so himself.) It was however more likely, they were also afraid of traversing the kitchen floor.

Lyn spent many nights trying – and failing – to get any recognition from his home nest for his efforts in promoting both them and the Caerphilly to his new friends across the kitchen floor. They were always glad to see him, taste the fresh, delicious Caerphilly but were equally shocked and disappointed at the attitude of Lyn's nest. In fact, they were also rather puzzled at such an attitude – they all looked after each other and mutually supported one another. How could a mouse who was doing so much good work for his own nest be spurned and treated with such disrespect by that nest?

Lyn, in his own way, and maybe conforming to his self-appointed role of eccentric, maintained his position as sole mouse ambassador for the Caerphilly cheese-eating nest. There were always some mice new not only to Lyn's story but also to the deliciousness of the Caerphilly and his educating them about his nest. One could tell from their starry eyes and smiling faces after Lyn's presentations (and the consumption of the cheese) that they had learnt new things, and that they had enjoyed these new experiences. Lyn therefore returned regularly to give further informative talks to his new friends.

However, Lyn could only reflect as he trotted home, alone, in the early hours of the morning after every such presentation, that a mouse is not without honour, save in his home nest. He permitted himself a bittersweet smile, greeted his parents gaily and promptly went to sleep, to dream of the following night and what he would do and say to the mice across the kitchen floor. They at least respected and appreciated him for himself.

35 An advisory letter to Scottish investors

31 January 2013.

Dear Scottish clients,

I am writing to you today as your financial adviser with a few ideas and to provide you with what I believe to be useful information when the time comes for you to invest in your future.

I note that there are two business concerns which may prove to be of interest to you, Alba Free plc and Yookay Ltd. I will set out some of the financial and other information that both these businesses are offering and I will then tender you my professional advice. This information will be presented in tabular form for ease of comparison.

Alba Free plc.	Yookay Ltd.
If you invest in this company, not only will you be a shareholder, treated equally with all other shareholders, you will be considered an absolute joint owner of this company	If you invest in this company you will remain a minority shareholder in the business, with little opportunity to speak up. You will not be treated as an equal in the company
As one of the equal shareholders and owners of the company you will have the power to vote in and vote off members of the company's Board of Directors	As a minority shareholder in the company you will have no right to appoint members of the company's Board of Directors.

	These will be appointed on your behalf by the majority shareholders who believe they are acting in your interests (but usually are acting in their own)
As one of the equal shareholders and owners of the company, you have a right to veto any contentious issue that arises from discussions arising from meetings of the Board of Directors In practice, this means you can refuse: - Prescription charges on your (by now) secure	As a minority shareholder, your voice will barely be heard when there are discussions at meetings of the Board of Directors (assuming the Board let you in, in the first place) In practice, this means: - Prescription charges will be re-introduced

National Health Service - Tuition fees on students in your universities - To retain Weapons of Mass Destruction in your home waters - To take part in illegal wars allegedly called in your name, but in reality based on terminological inexactitudes - Legislation	into the National Health Service, prior to the privatising of the whole of that Service - Tuition fees for all students will be set at market value – at whatever level the market dictates, with year on year increases above the level of inflation after that - Weapons of Mass Destruction

which is aimed at punishing the weakest members of society such as the unemployed and the disabled - To sanction further exports of precious oil to neighbours without adequate recompense for supplying it	will be kept within your waters and close to your centres of population so as to show the world that this one nation still has clout in the world - Punitive measures against the weakest members of society (*wassat?* Ed.) will be put into force and rigorously applied. You will be presumed in all cases to be

	available for work unless you are dead – in which case, gainful employment as a corpse in Agatha Christie murder productions must be actively sought*
- That the company has inalienable rights to your mineral wealth at all times and will seize them and pay you inadequately for their use (if at

	all)
You have the right to shares in the company to the value of £20.14 and you will receive an annual dividend from the company, paid by the Board of Directors, many of whom you will know personally and who will receive the same level of dividend as yourself	You have the right to shares in the company to the fixed value of £17.07

You have no right to a dividend at any time, as the only people to profit will be the anonymous Board of Directors |

(* The onus on finding a suitable role lies with the dead body. Otherwise your benefits will be cut.)

From the summary above, I think it is fair to say that when the opportunity arises for you to invest your money wisely, and I am confident that as canny Scots who are astute at money management, you will elect to invest in Alba Free plc. You may also be interested to know, as it is not widely reported in the media, that Yookay Ltd. is teetering on the brink of administration. This being the case, you would again, I venture to suggest, be well-advised in investing in Alba Free plc.

I trust I have been helpful with my advice to you today. May I wish you long life, good health and prosperity with your investments in Alba Free plc?

Should you require any further financial assistance, please do not hesitate in asking.

Yours sincerely,

B. Alan Sheet
Financial Adviser

36 Bunny's bid for freedom

Once upon a time, there lived a large, rather fat man called John West-Minster. He owned a little, fluffy rabbit called Bunny. Bunny lived in a rather small cage in John West-Minster's garden, and although she could see the expanse beyond her little cage, she was never let out to wander freely in the garden. Every day, John West-Minster would open the hutch door and throw in some old lettuce leaves for Bunny. Bunny was a docile animal and she remained faithful to her master.

One day John West-Minster came to Bunny's hutch with his usual offering of old lettuce leaves. Bunny wrinkled up her nose.

"I've had enough of your rotten old lettuce leaves," she said.

"Eh?" stammered John West-Minster. "You can talk? You have a voice, Bunny? I always thought you were a poor, dumb animal!"

"Yes, I can talk," replied Bunny. "And what is more, I've been quiet long enough."

"B-b-b-ut," stuttered John West-Minster. "Why now, Bunny? I've always given you green and healthy lettuce leaves. Why these are straight from Con Dem's greengrocers this morning. That nice Mr Osborne was behind the counter and he gave me these leaves for you. Look at the mark – Barnett brand. You can't aspire to any better quality than that."

"You can stuff your Barnett branded lettuce leaves, John," replied Bunny baring her teeth. "You know full well that if you examine those leaves that they really are of the lowest possible quality. There are holes all over them where little caterpillars and other insects have been feasting – long before I get a look in."

"But, Bunny. I love you. I'm concerned about you. I give you a good meal every day. I gave you this lovely hutch to spend your life in. What more could you ask for?"

"What more could I ask for?" said Bunny, her lip curling. "For a start you could vary my diet by giving me that juicy carrot that hangs up in Jenkins's Emporium in the High Street. But you won't do that – you think I should be grateful for those mouldy old lettuce leaves from those little shops in Union Street. Sometimes you go to the Con Dem's shop, another time it's lettuce leaves from old Ma Lamont's, another time you try to suggest that Davidson and Davidson's lettuce leaves are the best. Whereas in fact, they're all the same – lettuce leaves well passed their sell by date and leaving an unpleasant taste in the mouth."

"B-b-b-ut ..." said John West-Minster.

"And as for this hutch!" Bunny was in full control of the conversation now. "I get no chance to go anyplace outside of it. It's not natural, nor healthy, for an active, intelligent rabbit like me to remain cooped up here. And every day too! My cousins, out there in the country are free! Free, do you hear?" Bunny was shouting now. "That's the natural state for bunnies everywhere – not languishing in a small wire hutch subject to the whims of a surly and distinctly ungenerous master."

"But, Bunny," said John West-Minster, swallowing hard. "I've taken good care to give you food regularly over the years. I've cared for you deeply. It was me who built you this hutch. You know full well that you are too small, too fluffy and too insignificant to possibly survive by yourself if you were allowed to gambol with your cousins outside. I want you here so I can control you – I own you remember! You have no right to tell me how to look after rabbits."

"Yes, you've cultivated this image of me being soft

and cuddly and cute long enough, John," replied Bunny. "And I almost believed it myself too. But I've outgrown these things – I've learnt new things and I want to better myself! No more sweet, fluffy little Bunny here. I'm going to get that carrot from Jenkins's Emporium myself – and you're not going to stop me!"

"I have a good mind to thrash you with my Darling stick," roared John West-Minster. "Ungrateful little impudent rabbit. You're getting ideas above your station."

"Far be it from me to help you, John" replied Bunny defiantly, "But if you do that, all of my cousins will see you in your true light. A cruel, despotic master who is intent upon imposing his will on a small creature like myself. A creature who is only seeking that which is natural for all – freedom from outside malign influences and able to feed itself on the good things in life. I swear to you today, John West-Minster, I will escape this rickety, small and stultifying hutch and win for myself both that delicious carrot and my own freedom!"

"Harrumph!" growled John West-Minster. "We shall see! I hold all the trump cards: Biased Brutish Communications, the Campaign for Keeping Rabbits in their Allocated Places (CKRAP), all the mainstream media, the members of the British Association for Saving This Amazing Ruritanian Democracy (BASTARDS) and Bitter Together are all on my side. You have no chance against our combined might Bunny."

Bunny gritted her teeth. She knew that morality, decency and justice were on her side. She knew what she had to do. Liberation would be the antidote to her woes – and she would never have to stomach those meagre, awful lettuce leaves again. Bunny would make her escape plans carefully – she knew that if she were to fail, John West-Minster would reinforce the security on her hutch. It was more than likely that she would not have a better chance to put her aspirations into practice ever again. Bunny was committed to the cause of her personal freedom.

Dear readers, will Bunny be able to succeed and obtain that longed for carrot? Or will John West-Minster be able to thwart her bid for freedom and keep her incarcerated in an even more secure hutch – and on fewer lettuce leaves than before?

The story concludes in September 2014.

37 The Scott family trunk

Jack Union was an inveterate gambler. As often as not, he was to be seen in one of the many casinos in town. He was seldom seen in these places without his bosom pal, Sam Washington.

Like most gamblers, Jack Union lost more money than he won. But that did not stop his addiction to roulette, blackjack or slot machines. On the contrary, the more he lost, the more he would stake in the (often erroneous) belief that this outward appearance of riches would influence the roulette wheel or the card dealer and he would recoup (and with interest) his initial ante. Most of the croupiers had by now got wind of this piece of ostentatious bravado on the part of Jack Union, had seen it for the pretence of power or sham that it really was, and had happily arranged matters so that Jack Union would continue to lose money at their casinos. So it was then that Jack Union, and egged on by Sam Washington, could be seen squandering his money on the throw of a die or on the turn of a card night after night.

In fact, it would be charitable to say that Jack Union was throwing his own money about on the gaming tables and elsewhere. One might have allowed Jack Union the personal choice of frittering away his money. Maybe one might have suggested, very tactfully of course, that he seek counselling for his addiction. But, if rebuffed, a likely scenario as not, one could shrug one's shoulders, withdraw and walk on by. To each their own.

What was more pernicious however was that in fact, Jack Union was gambling away money that he held on trust for others. In so doing, he was not only breaking legal principles but also his moral obligations towards those others.

Some time previously, Jack Union's neighbours, the Scott family, had fallen on hard times. In order to raise some revenue they had been obliged to sell an old trunk which had been in the family for centuries and was considered to be a valuable heirloom. The trunk was therefore sold to the brokers, Purcell O. Rogues on Cabal Street in town. The sum realised was a meagre £17.07. Rogues had then sold the trunk on to Jack Union at a healthy profit to themselves, with the (and as it turned out, unenforceable) caveat that he, Jack Union, would look after the Scotts in any business dealings involving the trunk.

Now the trunk also came with a large amount of a thick, black and unpalatable liquid which was held in a vast number of bottles. Jack Union quickly seized the opportunity afforded to him by this and began to sell off the bottles of black liquid, thus making a big profit for himself. Obviously, monies accruing from the sales of this commodity were then "invested" in the casinos – not transferred to the Scotts as detailed under the trust deed. Thus, the profits fed Jack Union's gambling addiction and also underlined his illegal and immoral conduct as the Scotts' trustee and guarantor.

Naturally, the Scotts were not best pleased at Jack Union's behaviour. What they considered to be their birthright was being sold off in order to finance Jack Union's gambling lust. So they gathered together, decided to enlist the support of their friends, notably Jacob Ite and his dashing young lieutenant, Charlie Stewart, to petition Jack Union for the return of the trunk. To no avail. Redcotes, Jack Union's butler, refused them entry and gave Jacob Ite a bloody nose on the doorstep of Culloden House. Charlie Stewart was forced to flee for his life when Redcotes called for the enforcer, Butcher-Cumberland. (This last was known in town for his savagery and ferocity. Butcher-Cumberland was not a man to be trifled with nor crossed.)

Having dismissed Jacob Ite's petition out of hand, Jack Union reinforced his position and continued to act with impunity. When the trunk was not in use, he had it securely padlocked. Redcotes acted the dutiful retainer. A private army was maintained under Marshal-Wade to crush any future attempt by the Scotts to regain the historic trunk. In the legal domain, Messrs. Darling, Lamont, Davidson and Davidson (Solicitors and Commissioners for Oaths – the last named partner being well-known for administering oaths) spun legal principles in order to maintain Jack Union's authority over the Scotts, deprive them of the historic trunk and protect him from being sued for breach of the trust deed. (The other partner in this legal practice was said to be on sick leave. Contrary to popular belief, Rennies give you indigestion – not relieve you of it.) Jack Union therefore felt secure that nothing could hinder his progress to further profits and his enjoyment of gambling.

But as is often the case, nemesis is to be found to be a close companion of hubris. One evening, Jack Union lost a much larger sum than normal at the Iraq Venture casino. At his side, as was usual, was his best friend, Sam Washington. Now, subsequently, and although the link between the two was not proven, a few weeks later Jack Union was barred from the AAA Club. In private, he was furious at this slight to his seemingly invincible self-confidence. In public however, Jack Union insisted that there would be no change in his outward behaviour. He had to keep up appearances. He would continue to squ- – errmm – invest the monies earned from the sale of the bottles of the black liquid in other casinos.

The Scotts, quite naturally, were appalled by the man's brazenness. There had to be a way of reclaiming their historic trunk. They had to shock Jack Union into realising what he was doing and that like all gamblers and cheats he would ultimately be left all alone with no friends or money. Not that they felt any pity for him, of course – it had gone too far for that.

Yes. That was it. They, the Scotts, had to take matters into their own hands. They would have take the trunk back themselves. They would also get a Salmond key from Jenkins's the locksmiths on h-Aye Street in town. This key would serve as a skeleton key, opening any lock, removing any obstacle to their acquiring the trunk, and most importantly opening the padlock to the trunk itself which Jack Union had placed on it, once it had been returned home. The regaining of the Scott family trunk then would quite literally be in their hands.

Next, a date for the planned day for liberating the trunk from Jack Union's house had to be agreed upon. It was then unanimously accepted that 18 September was ideal – most of Jack Union's private army would be away on leave or square bashing at their annual muster in Aldershot or Brighton or Blackpool or wherever at that time. (It did not really matter where – it was enough to know that most of the Praetorian Guard as it were would be away then.) The Scotts and their followers would then be able to rush on Jack Union's house, seize the trunk and return both it and the bottles of black liquid back to their rightful owners.

An element of surprise was vital – Jack Union and his cohorts would not (nor indeed, should not) expect an attack. In order to avoid being seen by either Redcotes or Butcher-Cumberland or indeed PC Cameron, it was decided that the action to liberate the historic trunk had to occur at night. (They took their cue from the actions of a previous generation who had successfully carried off the Stone of Destiny just before eight o'clock – ten to eight or 19.50 to be exact – one Christmas Night.) The date, 18 September had been fixed. Watches were to be synchronised for a little before a quarter past eight, 20.14, on that evening.

Will the Scotts be successful in winning back their old family heirloom, their historic birthright and talisman as represented by the trunk and the bottles of black liquid? Will the trunk once more have pride of place in their home – its proper home? The family know that it is tantalisingly close to their grasp. They also know that if they fail that the retribution of Jack Union and his associates will be harsh and unmitigating.

They also know that if they succeed that they will be depriving Jack Union of his money making schemes at their expense. On learning of the loss of the trunk and the bottles of black unpalatable liquid, Jack Union will find he will no longer have the means of funding his once lavish and extravagant lifestyle. He will expire a bitter and twisted man. Jack Union's downfall and demise will not be lamented in the Scott household.

38 Mrs. Scott's aye test

Mrs. Scott was having her eyes tested.

"And what seems to be the problem, Mrs. Scott?" asked the optician.

"Well," said Mrs. Scott. "It's that just recently I haven't been able to see very clearly. I know there's a lot to see out there and to appreciate, but nothing seems to be easy to make out. Things tend to be rather blurred to me at the moment."

"Let me see if I can help you," smiled the optician.

The optician handed Mrs. Scott a pair of spectacles with a red, white and blue striped frame. Mrs. Scott put them on.

"These are our BT 001 model," said the optician. "Now, I'm going to hold up a card with some words on them. Tell me, Mrs. Scott. What can you read?"

"Errm," said Mrs. Scott, peering through the BT 001 spectacles. "I can see '*nuclear weapons*'. I can see the words '*social cuts,*' '*privatisation*' and '*poverty,*'" she said.

"Good," said the optician. "Now, let's try reading the letters on the board in front of you."

Mrs. Scott looked directly in front of her and began reading from the card.

"S-T-U-D-E-N-T errmm F-E-E-S," she spelt out.

"Very good," said the optician. Then he asked, "Can you see clearer with these BT 001 glasses, Mrs. Scott?"

"Oh yes, indeed I can," replied Mrs. Scott. "But have you anything else? These spectacles tend to weigh heavily on my nose."

"How about this pair then?" said the optician. He handed Mrs. Scott another pair of glasses. These had a blue frame with a large white cross. "This is the OI 180914 model," he said. "It's very popular at the moment." Mrs. Scott tried them on.

"Now, please read what is on the card, Mrs. Scott," the optician said.

"N-O eerrmm umm W-M-D," said Mrs. Scott. "And I can even read the line underneath too. That's, N-O um F-E-E-S."

"That's excellent!" cried the optician.

"Yes," said Mrs. Scott. "I wouldn't have been able to read all of that without these glasses!"

"Let's try another test," said the optician. "Can you read that word in the big circle, Mrs. Scott?"

"Oh, yes! That word is very clear to me. It says '*independence.*'"

"You have no doubts about that?" queried the optician.

"None at all!" smiled Mrs. Scott.

"Now, let's try that with the BT 001 model" said the optician, putting the first pair back onto Mrs. Scott's nose.

"Hmmm," said Mrs. Scott. "There's a very big difference. The first part of the word is very blurred now. I can't make it out at all. It's almost as if it's not there at all."

"So what can you see with these red, white and blue framed spectacles, Mrs. Scott?" asked the optician.

"I see '*dependence*,'" she replied. "Are you sure that it really says '*independence*'?"

"See for yourself," smiled the optician, giving Mrs. Scott the OI 180914 spectacles again. She took off the BT 001 glasses and replaced them with the others.

"Great heavens!" Mrs. Scott exclaimed. "It really *does* say '*independence*'! I can see so much better with these glasses – and more accurately too! It would be very dangerous of me to rely on these BT 001 glasses, don't you think?"

The optician smiled again.

"'*Independence*'! Yes! '*Independence*'!" Mrs. Scott was beaming from ear to ear.

"So which spectacles will you take, Mrs. Scott?" asked the optician.

"Definitely these ones," she replied, clutching the OI 180914 model. "They're much more comfortable to wear and make my vision much clearer and brighter too. I'll be able to look the world in the eye much better if I have these. I don't think there'll be much interest in your old BT 001 model either. I most certainly will have nothing further to do with them – and I'd advise you to bin them too!"

"They are useful to compare with the glasses you have chosen," said the optician. "By using both models I can let my customers decide for themselves. But, in truth, it's often an eye-opener for them when they can see how much better they can see with that model" he pointed to the the OI 180914 spectacles again in Mrs. Scott's left hand, "than with the BT 001 model."

"Thank you very much indeed for all your help and friendly advice," said Mrs. Scott. "I'm sure to recommend this pair to all my friends." She waggled her new glasses gently in her hand. "I might even suggest them to my acquaintances in London – they suffer badly from myopia, you know."

"And thank *you*!" replied the optician. He was smiling again. "You've made a very wise choice. The eyes have it!"

39 The racehorse and the beetle

There was once a racehorse called Alba Lassie who was kept in Union Stables. She was of a fine pedigree and would often take part in races on behalf of her rich owner. Her jockey wore the stables' colours of red, white and blue and he was not averse to using the whip; maybe sometimes more than was justified. Alba Lassie did not win that many races. Even when she did, she rarely received any recognition from her owner, other than a few pats to her flanks and perhaps some extra sugar lumps.

Alba Lassie was bemoaning her lot to herself inside her stable one day when she heard a small voice.

"What's that you say?" asked the small voice.

Alba Lassie looked down into the straw and saw a small gold and black beetle. The beetle returned Alba Lassie's stare.

"Who are you?" asked Alba Lassie, a little afraid that her talking to herself had been overheard.

"My Latin name is *Essenpius Victorius*," replied the beetle. "But that's a bit of a mouthful. You can call me Alex."

"O-o-ok," said Alba Lassie tentatively. "Have you been listening to me talking to myself?"

"I have," smiled Alex. "And I think your complaints are fully justified. Tell me what's worrying you and I'll see if I can help you."

"Please. You mustn't tell my owner then," said Alba Lassie. "I would probably be whipped harder if he ever got to know what I really thought."

"You have my word," said Alex. "If you are willing to confide in me, then I promise not to tell anyone."

"Well," began Alba Lassie rather cautiously. "It's like this. Firstly, I feel rather underappreciated at these stables. You know the white horse – Saxon Boy – in the adjoining stable?"

Alex nodded.

"It seems to me," went on Alba Lassie, "that every time he wins a race, he gets *far* more attention from the owner, the grooms and stable boys than when I win."

"Yes, I've heard you say that before," replied Alex.

"You've been eavesdropping on me before then?" asked Alba Lassie, a little concerned.

"Don't worry," answered Alex. "Everything you tell me will be kept in the strictest confidence."

"All right, then" said Alba Lassie. "I lack friends who I can talk to."

Alex smiled. "Go on," he said.

"I think the really big issue here is that I don't like being in these Union Stables anymore," said Alba Lassie. "Being made to jump those high fences on racecourses and being whipped to do so ..." she trailed off, and gave a shudder. "Why, to be honest with you, Alex, I don't think it's natural for us horses."

"I think you've some very good points there, Alba Lassie," said Alex. "And if you'll excuse the pun, I think you should run with them."

"I would," replied Alba Lassie, "but you see, my owner thinks I have a stable relationship with him here. (He can make bad puns too, you see.) And he would *never* countenance the idea of me ever leaving Union Stables – except perhaps as a tin of dog food or some cheap equivalent of beef for the humans."

"You know as well as I do," said Alex, "that your ancestors were always free. Free to roam the plains and not be accountable to any human. That was – and is – the natural state for horses. You should aim to reclaim the liberty of your forebears!"

"A fine sentiment," rejoined Alba Lassie. "But I can't see how I could possibly do it. You know that I'm under my owner's eyes practically all the time when I'm outside this stable. When I'm racing, my jockey in the red, white and blue livery has complete control over me. That's how and why he can get away with whipping me so hard!" Alba Lassie gave a loud whinny. "It's horrible!"

"Have you tried unseating your jockey?" asked the beetle.

"Oh, yes! I've thought about that many times," Alba Lassie gave a bittersweet smile. "Thought about it many times, but never had the courage to do so."

"I think there was a time during the 1979 Devo Stakes when you almost went close to succeeding, though." Alex smiled.

"Indeed," replied Alba Lassie. The bittersweet smile was still there. "But don't you remember, Alex, my jockey pulled hard on my reins that day and ensured that he didn't fall off?"

Alex nodded sadly.

"And I was whipped even harder when I got home that night, I can assure you!" Alba Lassie continued bitterly. "I was even threatened with being packed off to the dog meat factory that very night by my owner. As it was, I was whipped and deprived of my usual after-race carrots. All of that bloody well hurt, I can tell you!"

Alex was silent for a bit. Then he said, "You know, I'm an eternal optimist. I'm sure things will get better. Believe in yourself and there is no object that can stand in your way. I'll personally see you right too."

"Are you sure?" replied Alba Lassie, a little fearfully. "But," she went on, "I think I can trust you, Alex. Especially as I've told you all these things. Thank you for being such a good listener."

"Goodnight, Alba Lassie."

"Goodnight, Alex."

***

The following morning, Alba Lassie, Saxon Boy and all the other horses went out for their usual canter. It was a fine morning and all the horses were glad to be out of their stables in the fresh air. Saxon Boy was particularly happy – he was going to represent Union Stables at the Grand International that afternoon and his jockey would be sporting the red, white and blue livery.

As it turned out, the Grand International was a great success for Union Stables and its owner. Saxon Boy

– against all the odds – won the race and he was feted as a hero. His owner kept on slapping his flanks and saying what a magnificent thoroughbred he was. All the staff, the trainers, the grooms, the stable boys and the stable girls were to be complimented on ensuring that Saxon Boy was in such peak condition. The horse himself could be assured of further lavish attention and more treats than he could manage for the rest of his lifetime.

The news of Saxon Boy's victory of course permeated into the ears of the other horses. Most of the horses were pleased and even Alba Lassie forced herself to smile a little, before falling asleep later that evening.

However, her sleep was soon disturbed by a loud "Pssssssssssst!" in her ear. When she woke up she saw Alex, the gold and black beetle, sitting on the manger.

"Hello again, Alba Lassie," said Alex. "Great news about Saxon Boy, don't you think?" Alex bore no jealousies towards the horses whose stables he visited.

"Aye, right," replied Alba Lassie with a thin smile. "You said you'ld be sure things would get better. Well, they have – for Saxon Boy. Not for me!"

"Shush!" said Alex the beetle. "Things are better than you think. Tell me. What's stopping you from marching out of this stable now?"

"You know as well as I do, Alex," replied Alba Lassie. "My owner has put a padlock on the door. I can't possibly just gallop out of this stable into the fresh air by myself – no matter how much I want to."

"Ah." Alex was smiling. "But what if I told you that your owner and his friends and all the Stables' staff are having a big party at the house tonight to celebrate Saxon Boy's victory?"

"So?" Alba Lassie was unsure where this was leading. "So what?"

"Well," went on Alex. "What if I further told you that because of his drunken state, the chief groom, Cameron, has forgotten to padlock your stable door?"

"You mean ... ?" Alba Lassie was beginning to smile broadly.

"Yes. I mean one forceful kick of yours to the door from one of your hooves and the door will open ..."

"And I will be able to take up my freedom from Union Stables, once and for all!" finished Alba Lassie ecstatically.

"You've got it!" cried Alex.

"No more jockey telling me what to do! No more whippings! No more suffering the indignity of other horses taking the credit for my work! No more miserly after race sugar lumps – but my own treats and of my own choosing!" Alba Lassie was practically dancing with delight. "Freedom from Union Stables!" she cried.

"You've got it!" repeated Alex. "But remember, you won't get a better chance than tonight! You must seize this opportunity given to you. You have the chance to obtain those things you mentioned if you act promptly and without a moment's hesitation!"

Alba Lassie nodded.

"But if you don't take this golden opportunity," went on Alex, "you'll probably regret it all your life. Your stable door will be padlocked again as it has been on all previous nights. Your owner won't win the Grand International every year, nor go on a bender every night. He may well have spies who are already suspicious that you've been planning a break out from here for a long time. They would think nothing of informing on you to your owner." Alex paused. Then he said, "And you know what that will lead to?"

Alba Lassie sighed a deep sigh.

"Yes, I do," she said. "If I'm lucky, it will mean a securer stable. My staying here in Union Stables and getting more whippings and less food because I countenanced the idea of leaving. And ..." Alba Lassie gave a big shudder.

"And," Alex finished for her, "and if you're *unlucky*, a one-way ticket to the knacker's yard!"

"Oh, Alex!" Alba Lassie was almost crying. "Thank you for telling me all this! Thank you for being my friend!"

"You're very welcome," replied Alex. "But, remember. I'm only a facilitator in all this. The final decision on whether you take this opportunity to seize your freedom or not is down to you. I'm confident though that you'll do right for yourself and regain the liberty that once was the mark of your ancestors."

"Yes," smiled Alba Lassie. "I now know what I must do!"

40 Three men in a car

Once there were three men who worked together in a partnership. Their names were George, Andrew and David. As they were all based in the same office, it was decided that it was more practical to travel there in one car. George, being rather bossier than the other two partners insisted that he do the driving of all three of them in his car every day. Andrew would be in the front passenger seat and David would be in the back seat.

Now this arrangement did not really suit Andrew or David. Firstly, Andrew had rather long legs; he therefore felt a little cramped in the front passenger seat. He would have felt much better in the open air, free to stretch his legs and not be squashed into the small car that George owned. David, being in the back seat, was also rather displeased. He felt left out of any conversation between George and Andrew and often had to content himself by looking out of the windows during their journeys together. George, of course, was in control of the vehicle, and by extension, often thought of himself as being responsible for his passengers, Andrew and David. However, when it came down to it, you would find that rather hard to believe.

First of all, George's car had obviously seen better days. It had many miles on the clock and the engine tended to seize up on many occasions. This had led to many costly visits to the garage, where repairs were often made - repairs that in fact turned out to be merely cosmetic. Breakdowns of the car were frequent. The upholstery of the car was in a generally poor condition and the general upkeep left much to be desired. George did little to keep the car clean; there was mud over much of the paintwork (which of itself tended to hide large areas of rust) and the windows were very often opaque from the dust that George would pick up on his travels. Again, George's car was renowned for being very uneconomic. It was, truth to tell, a guzzler of fuel and therefore it was a pretty harmful vehicle to the environment. George had no time for what he called 'the green lobby.' Instead, he was more than happy to use the fossil fuels that were being extracted from the North Sea by a company Andrew held shares in. Further, owing to George's driving, and of which more presently, the vehicle had many dents in its bodywork where it had come off second best in the various scrapes it had endured with other road users.

George, as has already been mentioned was not the most careful of drivers either. His steering was decidedly erratic: one moment he was veering to the left with his steering wheel, at other times he would swerve to the right. Then George would curse the other road users aloud for their bad driving – it was never *his* fault. Similarly, when he went through the motions of gear changing, this feat was often accompanied by a loud screeching as George manipulated the gear stick. Then he would shout that the "bloody stick must be stuck" or some such. It was never *his* fault for failing to engage the mechanism correctly.

All these bad habits did not endear George to either Andrew or David of course. Initially, they were grateful to him for the lift to and from work every day, but over time, considering the condition of the vehicle and George's driving, they became more and more concerned about their own safety and well-being and were on the brink of refusing any further offers of lifts from him.

In point of fact, one day, Andrew had even attempted to seize the steering wheel from George and to place the car on a straighter path, when George had veered again to the right, when he alleged he had seen a Farage cow in his path. At that time, George and Andrew had exchanged a few choice words. Despite that, Andrew still lacked sufficient courage to tell George that he would never accept a lift from him again. David, in the back seat, as usual, kept a moody silence – he knew Andrew was right, and he would have applauded him had he decided to end his professional relationship with George. However, David himself was of the type who did not want to upset the apple cart and, knowing that he shared his office space (as well as the car) with George, felt that it was best to keep quiet – at least for the time being. Andrew, by contrast, had his own office within their partnership of three and had some greater degree of autonomy.

****

Then, one day, as they were travelling to work, with George driving as usual, they passed by Jenkins's Motors. There, on the forecourt, stood a gleaming, new blue and white car. Andrew was immediately impressed by what he saw.

"I'd love to buy that new car," he said.

"You can't do that," replied George. "I've been driving you to and from work for years now. How could you be so ungrateful after all this time?"

"I can't do that?" retorted Andrew angrily. "Who do you think you are? My mother?" Andrew was shouting. "How dare you treat me like a five year old!"

"You haven't got the wherewithal to buy that car," said George maliciously. "And you haven't driven for a long time. Look at me. I'm an accomplished and seasoned driver. You couldn't possibly be able to take to the road in that without causing some serious accident."

"Without causing some serious accident?" Andrew repeated scornfully. "I'll tell you what, George, we've been through a hell of a lot of scrapes with you already. And it's only by the grace of God – if you believe in that sort of thing – that we haven't had a really serious accident ourselves. Or even several!"

"He's right, you know," mumbled David from the back seat. But no one really took much notice of him. He would have to speak with a louder voice and gain more self-confidence before they did.

"And another thing," continued Andrew, the wind in his sails by now, "your vehicle is a death trap. The engine breaks down regularly. The paintwork is grimy and rusty. The windows are filthy. As often as not the windscreen wipers don't work. I'm not going to stand for it a moment longer."

"Why you ungrate–" started George.

"And as for your driving!" Andrew went on. He was obliged to get the resentments he had been feeling for years off his chest. "Heaven help us! Do you actually know what a gear stick is for? I'm sure you don't, considering the way this car complains each time you change gear. You steer this vehicle like a drunk, swerving from left to right and back again as if you're under the influence of the bottle. It's a wonder you haven't been caught and breathalysed by the police!"

"Why you impudent ..."

"Damn you and damn your car!" shouted Andrew. "I'm going to dissolve our partnership and buy that new blue and white car from Jenkins's Motors! I'll feel much better and safer when I'm behind the vehicle of my own choice and I'm in full control of the steering!"

"Well, bugger off then!" said George, stopping the car. "And don't come crawling back to me if you want a lift!"

"I won't need to," replied Andrew, smiling. "I have confidence that everything I need will be available to me when I take possession of my new car. I should have done this years ago!"

Andrew slammed the door and walked briskly towards Jenkins's car showroom. He knew what he had to do. He knew he had made the right decision.

41 Mr Scott and his bUNION

Mr Scott was in the doctor's surgery. He was a little anxious, but because of a pain in his left foot, he felt compelled to visit the doctor. Dr Jenkins had a reputation in the village of being a very sympathetic doctor who showed an active interest in the welfare of all his patients. Mr Scott felt he could trust Dr Jenkins and that the good doctor could alleviate the pain he was suffering.

"And what seems to be the problem, Mr. Scott?" queried Dr Jenkins, when Mr Scott's turn came.

"Well," said Mr. Scott, "It's that just recently I have been having these awful pains on my left foot. In fact, I feel the pain so deeply on my sole, that sometimes I can't walk very far because of the agony I'm in. I know that I should make the effort, I'm fearful that ATOS will punish me in some way, but really, doctor, the pain is so awful sometimes, I feel that I'm not going anywhere."

"Let me see if I can help you," smiled Dr. Jenkins. "Please take off your shoe and sock."

Mr. Scott did as requested and Dr. Jenkins bent down to look at the foot.

"Hmmm. Just as I thought, really," said Dr Jenkins. "You have a very unpleasant bUNION there, Mr. Scott. I think that needs coming out."

"I've heard of those" said Mr. Scott. "Don't they usually affect only ladies who have been wearing those high-heeled shoes?"

"I'm afraid that bUNIONS can and do affect all members of society," said Dr. Jenkins solemnly. "In fact, men and women, young people and old people all tend to suffer from bUNIONS. Sometimes they can last for many years. People are reluctant to see me, maybe out of embarrassment, but the facts remain the same. It's a very painful affliction, and as you've alluded to the fact itself, it can be potentially crippling and disabling."

"Yes, indeed, doctor," said Mr Scott. "I'm stagnating, staying at home in my armchair, when I should be out and about, seeing new things, taking part in new activities. This bUNION is ruining my life and I have every confidence that if you remove it for me, I will live a much more fulfilling life."

"Thank you, Mr Scott, for your confidence in me," said Dr Jenkins. "The procedure will be very simple, I can promise you. All I need is for your consent in using this Salmond scalpel™ on your foot, and I can guarantee you will be a new man."

"Anything you say, doctor," smiled Mr Scott.

Dr Jenkins rummaged in his cabinet and brought out the Salmond scalpel™.

"This might be a little painful at first," warned the doctor, "but once the action is done, you will never regret having this bUNION removed."

Then he started to apply the scalpel.

"Goodness, this bUNION is deep," Dr Jenkins said. "You must have been suffering from this for a long time!"

"Oh, yes indeed, I have, doctor," replied Mr Scott. "So long, that I almost can't remember. It must have been there in my youth."

"Too long," remarked Dr Jenkins. "But fortunately, we can still remove it."

And with that, wielding the Salmond scalpel™, Dr Jenkins cut out the nasty and painful bUNION.

"Now you will feel a few growing pains to start off with," said Dr Jenkins, "but these will soon go away. How do you feel now, Mr Scott?"

"To be honest, doctor, I fell rather numb," replied Mr Scott. "But I'm sure that I will feel much better very soon, thanks to you."

"Well, it's not really me" Dr Jenkins said modestly. "It was really down to you coming to see me about your painful affliction. I am, as a doctor, only a facilitator in helping my patients get over their aches and pains."

"I can't thank you enough though, doctor," Mr Scott said. "I must admit that in removing that bUNION I will now feel more inspired. I will become a far better athlete and getting to grips with my new found freedom will also improve my education. When you have no chains that bind, your options are limitless and the pain and the indignity of not being able to stand on your own two feet are an ancient memory."

"Go forth my friend," smiled Dr Jenkins. "Go, and tell all those of your compatriots that you have had your bUNION removed – so that they may feel the happiness in having theirs removed. Tell them that you are feeling far better as a result and additionally that your future prospects are far better than previously. Say YES to a far less painful and crippling future – one that keeps you shackled to your home and not enabling you to go forward with joy in your heart. Say YES to a bUNION free future!"

42 The shark and the turtle

"Hey there, sluggard!" said the Darling shark one day. "How slow, plodding and stupid you are! Look at me, little turtle, I can cruise the ocean currents swiftly and spread my negative message far and wide – before you're even out of your shell! The whole ocean is in awe of my power!"

"Perhaps," replied the little turtle. "But do you know what? The humans find your appearance worrisome and terrifying. That's why they've set out nets to trap you. Ultimately, they'll destroy you."

"Pah!" said the Darling shark. "Weak, insignificant thing that you are! What do I care for your opinion? I should by rights eat you here and now so that no one can hear your silly opinions!"

"Try it and see!" retorted the turtle. "You'll find that over time we turtles become immune to predators, because as we grow older, our shells get thicker!"

The Darling shark swam away, huffing and puffing, muttering threats against the turtle population. So engrossed was he in this personal rant, that he swam straight into a net laid by the humans. The humans immediately harpooned the shark. He was gutted that very night.

The turtle continued to bob happily among the waves along with his friends. He knew that his calm approach would ensure his own survival into a contented old age.

43 Angela Alba's having a baby

Angela Alba lives in a small town, not so far away and she's having a baby. Of that, there's no doubt. All the tests on her white paper checklist have proved positive, and now, nine months down the line, she knows she's going to give birth to a new life form. It's all so very exciting, and Angela's feeling pretty excited too. It will be a momentous day in her life and she knows it will change her perspectives and her ways of thinking forever. She also knows that after so many years of domestic abuse, she will finally be very happy. Angela has made a vow to herself and her unborn baby that she will do everything in her power to love him (or her) with as much mother's love as she can. The baby will want for nothing and Angela will ensure that it gets all that it needs in support to ensure that it will stand proud on its own two feet and look the world straight in the eye.

These last few years have been a trial for Angela. Her husband, Jack Union (Angela had at least kept her dignity and her maiden name on marrying – but little else) is an abusive, boorish, uncaring man. He has often left Angela in the lurch by going on various booze-fuelled trips with his mates, in particular Sam Washington. Many is the time that Angela has heard that they've been involved in fights at various pubs – the latest one being a fracas in the *Baghdad Arms*. It came as no surprise to Angela that both Jack and Sam were no longer welcome at the *Baghdad Arms* – they've been banned from so many other pubs in town. Even the patience of the landlady of *the European* pub, Bea Russell, is wearing a bit thin, and she's on the verge of issuing a final warning to Jack Union, before excluding him entirely from her hostelry.

Invariably too, Jack Union is an aggressive, selfish man. He keeps most of the money that he earns from Angela in order to maintain his boozy, self-centred lifestyle. He rarely gives anything to her. Indeed, so uncaring is he towards his partner, that Jack Union is not averse to taking *her* money too, leaving Angela poor and upset at home. Far too often, Angela is also the victim of domestic violence at the hands of Jack Union.

Angela has thought of leaving her abusive husband on many occasions. In 1979, she attempted to break free of him, but through a cunning ruse and frightening her into thinking that she couldn't live without him, Jack Union 'persuaded' Angela to stay.

Then, in 1997, after years of neglect, Jack bought Angela a new kitchen. Doubtless, he thought he was being very magnanimous towards his wife. But Angela saw things differently. Yes, the kitchen was a boon, it was a place of her own where she could do her own thing and think her own thoughts, but in reality it only served as a place where she could continue cooking and slaving for her husband. She was not truly free of his influence even then, not independent, and invariably if Angela did something wrong in the kitchen – burning Jack's toast, for example – Jack would bawl at her for being 'too weak, too poor, too stupid.' She couldn't even get such basic things right, he'd shout. He would then storm out of the house and join Sam Washington in a local bar and get drunk, all the while decrying Angela.

Angela is by now convinced that her relationship with Jack Union has broken down irretrievably. Their partnership is no longer one of two equals – if it ever was. She wants a divorce and she wants one quickly. But she's also sensible enough to realise that she has to insist on her fair share of the assets of their marriage. She has consulted her good friend, Nicola, a specialist in family law, and she has advised Angela how best to go about it. Although she's now pregnant, Angela can't see that the baby will change anything or bring both her and Jack Union together. It's gone too far for that, and indeed, knowing her husband's behaviour, Angela's aware that he didn't want this baby.

Jack Union is associating with Beattie, who has made a name for herself as 'the village bike.' She takes on all-comers, though it seems that Jack Union is her favourite 'client.' She's a crabby, embittered woman (not unlike her sisters, Johann and Margaret) and is jealous of the fact that Angela Alba's pregnant. Her own son, George London, has gone south and made a name for himself as a banker someplace in the City, where he has retained many of his mother's egotistical characteristics. He has never given the town a second thought since as he has pursued his own selfish goals – but he has retained the affections of and for his mother,

Beattie. This is only to be expected, but Beattie and her son still seem to be linked by an invisible umbilical chord, years after the latter's birth.

Beattie will have strong words with Jack Union about Angela's forthcoming delivery. There are those in the little town who whisper darkly that Beattie and Jack are already conspiring to ensure that Angela abort the foetus before the end of her term or that they are trying to induce her to miscarry. There must be some truth in this, as both Jack Union and Beattie are often to be seen leaping out of the shadows, projecting fear onto poor Angela.

But Angela is a resilient character. And aided and counselled by her good friend and lawyer, Nicola, who along with other members of the latter's legal partnership of Jenkins, Canavan and Salmond LLP, she's helping Angela maintain her dignity through it all. Angela Alba will stand tall, look the bullies in the eye, give birth in nine months' time to a bonny, wee baby, divorce her husband and make a new life for herself and her offspring. The rest of the little town will be *so* happy for her – she will truly be an independent woman, and be free of the machinations of her soon to be ex-husband, Jack Union. Both he and Beattie will be run out of town.

44 Reverend Caledonia and the candles

Reverend Caledonia had officiated at St. Alba's church for many years. The minister came into his church one morning, shivering. It was a cold morning and Reverend Caledonia, being rather elderly tended to feel the cold more than most. That morning however, he felt the cold outside more than usual – and he felt it in his church too. Something was not right, and Reverend Caledonia knew it.

Now, not only was Reverend Caledonia's church colder than usual that morning, the minister felt sure that it was darker too. He looked around him. It was then that Reverend Caledonia's gaze fell on the altar. He immediately saw what was wrong: his big altar candle, a venerable MacDonald taper which had served him and his congregation for a good many years had seemingly disappeared.

Reverend Caledonia hurried over to the altar, fearful that someone had stolen the MacDonald candle. When the minister arrived at the candlestick which held the candle, he realised what had happened. Far from being removed, the MacDonald candle had in fact completely melted and had gone out. Only its burnt and frayed wick and a small pool of wax remained as testimony to its former glory. Reverend Caledonia realised with a heavy heart that it would not be possible to relight the MacDonald candle.

When Reverend Caledonia took in this dreadful news, he fell to his knees and began to sob deeply and audibly. He began entreating God to give safe passage to the soul of the MacDonald candle. Now you may think this kind of behaviour a little bizarre – to feel such profound grief for something seemingly inconsequential and inanimate as a candle. But you have to appreciate that Reverend Caledonia was a very sensitive man. In all the years he had been the minister at St. Alba's he had developed some sort of affinity or connection with his altar candle.

The MacDonald candle had indeed come to symbolise, in true Christian fashion, "the light of the world," and it (or as Reverend Caledonia had personalised the candle over the years, "she") had given off light and warmth during his many services at St. Alba's. Reverend Caledonia knew that his congregation had also appreciated the light and the warmth the MacDonald candle had given off – and they too would miss that when they learnt that she was no more.

When Reverend Caledonia realised this fact, he sobbed all the louder. No other candle would (or indeed, could) replace the MacDonald candle – she was truly one of a kind.

But Reverend Caledonia was also a very practical and resourceful man. After a few minutes of silent contemplation, he dried his eyes and blew his nose a couple of times. He got up off his knees gingerly and started to smile.

He knew what he had to do and what his parishioners would expect him to do. So Reverend Caledonia began to light a number of little candles all over the inside of St. Alba's church. Now, as individual, little candles, they could in no way compare with the MacDonald candle – she was truly unique. They also lacked the experience she had in serving Reverend Caledonia in his services. But Reverend Caledonia also knew that the combined strength of the little candles – their joint giving of light and warmth – would help dispel the darkness and gloom inside St. Alba's. The little candles would also gladden the hearts of Reverend Caledonia and his parishioners.

And so it was that Reverend Caledonia, realising this little miracle of deliverance, again fell to his knees on the altar steps and gave thanks to God and expressed his gratitude for the work of the MacDonald candle. He also thanked God for inspiring him to continue her warm and joyful message through the medium of the little candles.

It would be a fitting tribute to the work previously carried out by the MacDonald candle and he was happy to be a facilitator in that process.

45 Georgia and Andrea

Georgia and Andrea were two of the most competitive mothers in town. They were as often as not to be seen arguing with each other over some matter or other in the street. Most of the other inhabitants of the town on such occasions would roll their eyes or sigh deeply and mutter to each other that "those two are at it again."

Now as befits any such competitive mothers, this was reflected in their offspring, in this case their daughters who attended the local secondary school. Georgia's eldest, Elizabeth, had latterly just completed her role as the latest Head Girl and had subsequently gone on to University. There was therefore a vacancy for the position of Head Girl at the school. Naturally, Georgia and Andrea were at each other's throats as to who the new Head Girl should be. (The quiet, demure Davida might well have proved a good compromise candidate but, in reality, her passivity, would have played against her. In any case, neither Georgia nor Andrea would have taken her candidature seriously. Davida herself was too much in thrall of Georgia in any case to even suggest putting her name forward in the first place.)

Then inspiration came from another source. Andrea's daughter, Jamie, put her own name forward, independently of her mother. She proposed that she should be Head Girl, but on condition that she would obtain extra tuition and help with her homework from Georgia who taught at the school. Jamie was rather tired of her mother and Georgia bickering all the time and thought this might be a way of calming both mothers down.

Georgia and Andrea reluctantly agreed and initially,

the agreement seemed to work well. Jamie was duly appointed Head Girl. Georgia revelled in the idea of being Personal Tutor to her. Andrea basked in the glory of her daughter's academic and social progress, although she was now paying her old foe for her daughter's lessons. Jamie herself began seeing a boy called Jack Union.

Then Jamie too moved up to University. The school management soon realised that the arrangement whereby the Head Girl was appointed having worked successfully in Jamie's case, decided to follow the same procedure for the subsequent one. A peace of sorts had broken out between Georgia and Andrea, and the school were keen that this should be maintained. So they made Andrea's second daughter, Charlotte, Head Girl. Charlotte would also have Georgia as her personal tutor, this ensuring that the other mother was not snubbed. Andrea gritted her teeth, but was sufficiently placated that Charlotte was maintaining the family honour as Head Girl and consented to the idea. Georgia too, despite not having a family member as

Head Girl, saw the financial advantages to herself in being Charlotte's personal tutor.

However, one day, a shocking event occurred. A strapping lass at the school, Olive by name, physically attacked Charlotte in the school playground. Charlotte's injuries were so serious that she was rushed to hospital where she later died. This news in itself was shocking enough and initially everyone was at a loss as to what to do. All except Olive of course.

Olive saw the opportunity that now presented itself to her. She had probably been planning this for some time, and biding her time to attack. Olive's father was a senior Governor at the school, and after a timely period of grief at the events in the playground, he strong-armed his fellow Governors into accepting Olive as the new Head Girl. (He convincingly persuaded them that Charlotte had actually provoked his daughter and that Olive had in fact only acted in self-defence.) Be that as it may, Olive was duly appointed Head Girl.

Her period in that position can at best be called 'puritanical.' The school Christmas Disco was cancelled as were 18th Birthday parties for students, previously organised by the students themselves. Olive decreed a new form of school uniform be worn by everyone; one which was a sombre black from head to toe.

It was with great joy then when Olive moved on to University and Charlene replaced her as Head Girl. Bright colours came back in and the Christmas Disco restored. Now, although Charlene was a gifted student and she attempted to restore reconciliation between Andrea and Georgia, in reality, she did little more than acknowledge their respective positions, in much the same way her predecessors, Jamie and Charlotte had done. Olive's reign as Head Girl had been a 'blip' and it was thought that a return to the status quo ante was deemed to be the best policy. Charlene however, was not averse to playing Georgia and Andrea against each other as the need arose, but stopped short of abusing either of them directly.

After Charlene had gone on to university, she was replaced by Jacqueline as Head Girl. Jacqueline quickly established herself as a deeply unpopular Head Girl. Like Olive before her, she had strong beliefs and sought to impose them on the rest of the school. She was not however a Puritan – far from it – but her pursuit of spreading her conviction of the universalist approach created many enemies. The school governors began to think it had been a mistake appointing Jacqueline as Head Girl, and they also thought she had pretensions of over-ruling all their decisions. It was with this in mind, that an emergency meeting of the governors was called, and Maria was to be invited to take over the position of Head Girl from Jacqueline.

Maria duly assumed the position of Head Girl, and in a unique settlement, insisted that she share her duties with her girlfriend, Billie. The school governors readily agreed and gave their support to Maria when the latter had a contretemps with Jacqueline on Boyne's field during a hockey match.

Jacqueline was sent off during that match, and having now lost the Head Girl's position and her dignity was obliged to retire to the sidelines. She therefore took it upon herself to go and live with her boyfriend, Francis.

Maria and Billie shared the duties of Head Girl between them. There was no going back to the policies that Jacqueline had pursued when she was Head Girl. Limitations on the powers of future Head Girls were set out in a written document for the first time, as were the extent of the powers accorded to the school governors and they were to be elected. No longer could the Head Girl decide things all by herself, and the governors could limit her power at any time. It was also decided that a similar document would be drafted for members of the 6th form so they would have the same standing as the rest of the school vis-à-vis the Head Girl's new role. The 6th form had now however to swear allegiance to Maria and Billie (and subsequent Head Girls) as part of this settlement by the beginning of the next academic year.

Some of the other girls were convinced however that the 6th form would not accept this new scheme of loyalty to Maria and Billie. One such was Dolly Rymple, who was Mistress of Stair House in the school. She therefore arranged with Billie that some sort of punitive action should be taken against those who did not. Disappointingly for Dolly, initially almost all of the 6th form gave their allegiance within the time limit. Only one girl did not, and that by accident and not purposefully. Her name was Glenys Coe, and she preferred to be known by the short form of her first name. Glen Coe had left it to the last minute to swear her allegiance to Billie and Maria – the end of the academic year was fast approaching when she presented herself at the school reception desk to do so on the last day of term. The temping secretary at the desk informed Glen that she had no power to accept her (Glen's) oath of allegiance and sent her away.

Glen now realised that her only option was to visit

the Headmistress in order to sign her allegiance – and that it would be after the deadline. She called upon the Headmistress at home, and, although Glen was allowed to swear her oath, both women knew it was invalid.

It was then that the Mistress of Stair House acted. She put it into Camilla "Cammy" Bell's (Glen Coe's classmate), head that Cammy should persuade Glen to invite her (Cammy) to a sleepover at Glen's. Cammy would then at the appropriate time receive a text message, from the Mistress of Stair House, approved of by Billie herself, that Glen should be taught 'a severe lesson for her disobedience.'

Cammy followed the instructions to the letter. Poor Glen was unaware she was letting in a viper into her home. When the appointed time arrived the following morning, Cammy turned on her hostess and strangled her in her own bed. These events shocked the whole community – except, perhaps Dolly Rymple, who expected things to return to the status quo ante, but even she was forced out of her position of Mistress of Stair House, eventually. The murder of Glenys Coe and the abusing of trust that she had put in Cammy Bell remained ingrained in school memory for a long time after these horrifying events had taken place.

It was only when Anna became Head Girl some years later that there was a significant sea change. Anna was cunning and a master tactician. She was fed up with the low-key sniping that continued between Georgia and Andrea, despite the work carried out since Jamie's time as Head Girl. So Anna contrived of a plan: Georgia and Andrea would enter into a civil partnership with each other – ostensibly as equals – whereby she (Anna) would receive love and respect from them both. Likewise, Andrea and Georgia would be bound by their signatures on the piece of paper that bound them to that civil partnership and make a success of their union. Anna considered this to be a win-win situation as far as she was concerned, and that it would put a definitive end to the friction between Andrea and Georgia, once and for all.

And so, and with some cajoling, bullying and influencing (some would say bribery), Andrea and Georgia's families were both persuaded to give assent to the civil partnership. The couple themselves, in an attempt to bury the hatchet, smiled for the cameras and declared their undying love for each other.

Andrea and Georgia's union however, did not get off to an auspicious start. Georgette (a German girl) had by then replaced Anna as Head Girl of the school and she was willing to do anything to undo the couple's civil union. The same could be said of her successors as Head Girl: Georgie, Georgina and Georgiana. During Georgina's tenureship of Head Girl, the school suffered two great calamities. First of all, Georgina had heavily invested school funds in a colonial venture in the Americas. The colonists themselves had found that this imposed great disadvantages upon themselves – to be polite, one could say that they thought of Georgina's meddling in their affairs as not their cup of tea. So, what started out like what appeared a mere storm in a teacup in Boston, quickly spread throughout the Colony until Georgina's flag was withdrawn completely from the territory. This was a terrible blow to the school – but much worse was to follow. Whether related to this fact or not, Georgina developed the signs of some form of insanity. This situation could not be tolerated amongst those who aspired to be Head Girls, and Georgiana was quickly drafted in to take onboard the day-to-day running of school affairs and to take charge of the other schoolgirls.

But we are jumping ahead of ourselves a little. There were still members of Andrea's family not reconciled to Andrea and Georgia's union. First there was Frances (who probably had aspirations on being Head Girl herself.) Then, later, there was Charlene-Edwina Stewart and her boyfriend Jacob Ite who tried to petition the authorities into annulling the civil partnership. On both occasions that both Frances and Charlene-Edwina attacked, they were repulsed by the powers that be. In the latter case, Butcher-Cumberland (a man known for his ferocity) gave Charlene-Edwina Stewart and Jacob Ite a bloody nose on the steps of Culloden House. As Charlene-Edwina fled the scene, she could hear Butcher-Cumberland's words bellowing in her ears: "If I ever see you again, I'll kill you!"

It was also during Georgina's tenure of the position of Head Girl that Georgia and Andrea allowed another lady to attend their coffee mornings. Patricia, for that was the lady's name, was made welcome by both of the others (it will be remembered that Davida kept a gloomy silence in the background, eclipsed by Georgia.) Patricia soon learnt that her place in pecking order was subservient to Georgia, but being a fiery redhead, she was not going to take this lying down. She regularly had bitter arguments with Georgia, and they often were one step away from exchanging physical blows with each another. It was really only a question of time before Patricia would storm out of the house, never to return. But even when she had done this, with fireworks and tears on both sides, part of Patricia's character was still in the thrall of Georgia, and she could be seen sometimes poking her face round the corner of the door in the hope of a quick cuppa and an Eccles cake.

After Georgiana had moved on to university, the vacancy of Head Girlship was filled by Wilma. She had a great interest in sailing boats and the sea, and behind her back, Wilma was often referred to as the "Sailor Queen." Everyone thought of her as not being particularly academically gifted, and that instead of going to university when she left school that she would more likely land herself a career in the Royal Navy. And that is precisely what happened – and her place as Head Girl was then given to Vicky.

Vicky packed a lot of adventures into her role as Head Girl. She expanded the school's interests in India and Africa and took Georgia, Andrea, Patricia (and Davida) with her. She promoted the more industrious girls to work harder at their studies, and both the needlework and cookery classes boomed as a result. She even encouraged like-minded girls to 'employ' their classmates in such ventures – some calling this entrepreneurship; others referred to it as exploitation and the use of cheap labour. Throughout it all, Vicky stood proud and aloof – and the term 'Vicky's Values' for such behaviour and the condoning of the aforementioned 'industrial' practices whilst seeking out further profit margins in Asia and Africa quickly caught on. Depending on who you asked, 'Vicky's Values' were positive in enriching the school and the wealthy girls or were negative as they impoverished the poorer girls still further and also exploited others overseas.

Edith, Vicky's successor as Head Girl, had already made a name for herself, even prior to elevation to that role. Rumours circulated about her that she was the school nymphomaniac and had had many boyfriends before she settled down with her more consistent boyfriend, Alex. That said, despite being attached to Alex, their relationship must surely have been a very open one – for Edith continued to dally with other boys whilst still remaining seemingly true to Alex. It must have been an enormous strain for him personally, but Alex smiled through it all, and was seemingly content to play second fiddle and to reflect in part in the glory of his partner's status as Head Girl.

Once Edith had moved on to university, the new Head Girl, Georgine, was appointed. Georgine's situation as Head Girl, like that of Georgina's before her, was marked out by certain key events, though, fortunately for Georgine herself, this did not cause her to suffer from any sort of mental collapse. First, there was the dispute between herself and her German cousin, Wilhelmina over which of them was the stronger of the two. It was only after some weeks of attrition between the two that it was finally decided that Georgine was the victor. But the relationship between her and

Wilhelmina had been soured – perhaps, permanently. Secondly, another cousin, Nikki, had been beaten up so badly by a gang of local red shirted yobbos that she eventually died from her wounds. A whispering campaign began against Georgine that she should have done more to help Nikki, and even to have allowed her to stay at her house whilst her injuries were being treated. Whether these rumours were based on truth or not it is impossible to say. What is certain is that Georgine's position was weakened as a result and the feelings of respect for her as Head Girl were diminished as a result.

Edie became Head Girl once Georgine had passed on to university and immediately found herself in the middle of a personal scandal. She was caught one day behind the bike shed with Wallace, a well-known rake and ladies man. The school was in uproar and Edie was forced to resign the position of Head Girl immediately.

Georgyann was originally called Bertha and was to

be the next Head Girl. During her stint as Head Girl, Georgyann had a contretemps with another girl, Adolpha. This proved to be just a serious dispute – if not worse – as between Georgine and Wilhelmina, and there are those who maintain that were it not for the active help of her friend, Samantha 'Sam' Uncle, Georgyann would not have won the day. As it was, Sam Uncle came into the argument between the two girls much later, but owing to the fact she was a much more muscular individual than either of them, she helped in defeating Adolpha. Georgyann's position would now be much more diminished as she had to depend on Sam helping her out more and more often and it immediately became apparent that Sam was jockeying for the lead position herself. What with the school also losing much of its ventures in Asia and Africa during Georgyann's tenure of the position of Head Girl, things looked bleaker still for the school. Georgyann duly went on to university and was succeeded by Lizzy.

Lizzy the new (and current Head Girl) has overseen further changes at the school. The loss of ventures abroad, in particular, Asia and Africa, have continued apace. Very soon, it seems as if all that Lizzy will be in charge of as Head Girl is the school itself.

Now let us return to the initial civil partnership between Andrea and Georgia. As part of this civil partnership, as part of Andrea's dowry in fact, she had brought with her many bottles containing a dark, unpleasant smelling and opaque, black liquid. When Georgia learnt of this, she immediately seized the bottles for herself. She then sold them at a high profit, which she then dissipated in wild, extravagant living. If Andrea was expecting a share of such profit, she would be sadly mistaken. Poor Andrea was often left in the house to herself whilst Georgia lived the high life in style. Salt was often then rubbed into her wounds when Georgia commented that she (Georgia) was actually subsidising Andrea.

True, Georgia did take the opportunity of taking Andrea on holiday to exotic places with her quite often: India, Aden, Kenya to name but three. But it was also true that some sort of jinx afflicted Andrea when they went to these places. It was always Andrea who went down with malaria or Delhi Belly or, as in South Africa, she broke her ankle. Georgia however would often survive such experiences with barely a scratch.

Now Andrea and Georgia are rather elderly ladies. Old age is creeping up on them and they are travelling less and less. In fact, truth to tell, they are less welcome in the places they went to previously than before – not that the locals really enjoyed their domineering style (particularly Georgia's) at the time. They are therefore obliged to be more and more in each other's company. They therefore have also more time to dwell on the memories of their youth. Andrea is still smarting from the ill-treatment meted out to her and her family post the civil partnership ceremony. She feels less and less of an equal in the partnership with Georgia in any case. Andrea is beginning to think it is time to stand up to Georgia and her bullying attitude once and for all.

With this in mind, Andrea has now consulted her lawyer, Nicola who is the family law specialist at Salmond, Canavan and Jenkins LLP in order to instigate proceedings to dissolve the civil partnership between herself and Georgia. Georgia, naturally, on hearing of this is caught in a rather Janus-like situation. She says she loves Andrea and promises her all manner of goodies, if only she will stay with her. Yet there is nothing tangible to these promises, and Andrea suspects that they are merely soft words from Georgia that will not materialise into anything concrete.

Again, at other times, Georgia will get into a rage and accuse Andrea of wanting to take back those black liquid containing bottles; bottles that have hitherto funded Georgia's lavish lifestyle. At these times, Georgia is angry with Andrea and insist that Andrea could not possibly survive without her help, when she reverts to being single.

To prevent the split occurring, Georgia too has engaged a lawyer, Alistair from the firm of McDougall, Lamont, Davidson and Davidson LLP. (The other partner, Rennie is currently on sick leave. Contrary to popular belief, Rennies give you indigestion, not relieve you of it.)

The decision of the court and the judgement of Mr Justice Scott in this case, due to be delivered on 18 September 2014, is eagerly awaited by all parties.

46 The flowers in Jon Bull's garden

Jon Bull had a garden and it was his pride and joy. In this garden, he did not grow any vegetables. He much preferred cultivating flowers that gave off sweet fragrances on the air. The main type of flower that Jon Bull was interested in were roses, and these were by far the most prolific flowers in his garden and he tended them with care. Jon Bull always ensured that they had sufficient water from his red, white and blue watering can. He gave them the best plant food. He nurtured his roses so well, that very soon they became the best-looking flowers in the whole garden.

The roses' roots were deeply secured and this enabled them also to seize the best nutrients from the ground – often at the expense of the other flowers in the garden. If they had feelings, they would surely have felt very happy, if not indeed a little smug about their position in Jon Bull's garden. They were the centre of attention in that garden and that was that. Every other flower was to be looked down upon through the roses' petals.

Now next to the roses, a smaller group of daffodils grew in Jon Bull's garden. These were a strange sort of flower. For although they grew in Jon Bull's garden, they had not been fully domesticated by him – they still tended to grow wild, and slightly apart, although, believe me, Jon Bull had attempted to turn them into more 'garden' than 'wild' flowers. As a form of spite perhaps, Jon Bull had therefore not thought it appropriate (perhaps 'worthwhile' would be a better word) to spend too much time and attention in cultivating the daffodils. In any case, as previously mentioned, the roses took up most of his time and attention, and some semi-savage, undomesticated daffodils were not really important enough to be treated in the same way as they were. The daffodils only bloomed for a short time anyway and it was not worth the effort to cultivate them as prodigiously as the roses – at least, that's how Jon Bull thought. It would also, he thought, lead to him neglecting his prized roses – something he could not and would not ever contemplate.

So the daffodils would bloom at the appropriate time, with, if we are to continue the feeling metaphor, a certain amount of sadness. Not for them the care given to the roses, and they would soon wither away. True, Jon Bull occasionally gave them some water from his red, white and blue watering can, but the amount was not really that significant. Yet, somehow or other, year in year out, the daffodils would still be there. And in early March, their resplendent trumpets were almost a match for the all-powerful roses.

Now adjoining the flowers in Jon Bull's garden were the thistles. By rights, Jon Bull thought of these plants as weeds, and an annoyance and menace to him, and indeed to his whole garden. In that capacity, they proved even more of a distraction and a more dangerous one in fact to his roses. Jon Bull had often tried to remove the thistles from his garden but had never succeeded. He first thought that removing the thistles by hand would be an easy enough task. But he soon found himself covered in painful prickles. As a result, he had to go home pretty quickly and to think on another idea of removing the thistles.

On other occasions, eschewing the use of his hands, Jon Bull had taken up his best patent Wastemonister™ spade in order to dig up the thistles by the root. But it was hard, strenuous work – the thistles' roots were deeply embedded – and it was often the case that Jon Bull had to give the task up, with sweat pouring from his red, fleshy face and his large stomach wobbling.

The thistles then would have resisted for another day. Indeed, they were able to proliferate further, as when their flowers had disappeared, their light, feathery seeds could be taken up by the wind and be dispersed all over. When these seeds came to land, they would germinate, and new, sturdy thistle plants would start growing – causing further consternation and anxiety to Jon Bull.

Another solution presented itself to Jon Bull in an effort to subdue the thistles – weed killer. He convinced himself that a good dose of Cullodenine™ would destroy the thistles once and for all. All his attention in dealing with them had been distracting him from attending to his beloved roses. Cullodenine™ would see an end to those troublesome thistles. However, although a lot of the thistles were killed as a result of the application of the Cullodenine™, in the long run, the weed killer actually proved quite ineffective. Enough of the thistle seeds had managed to escape the carnage, and had been seized by the wind to begin new journeys in the air oceans before falling to earth and germinating a new generation of thistles.

In due course, these new thistles established sturdy roots and stems which became resilient against anything Jon Bull could throw at them; be they his Wastemonister™ spade or a new, seemingly stronger weed killer, such Beeteeyuk™ which its salesman Darling had mistakenly convinced Jon Bull would be the most effective weed killer yet against those troublesome thistles. As for the thistles themselves, they had started to cluster together, knowing that their own common unity of purpose would repel both Jon Bull and any efforts to get rid of them. They also grew stronger prickles in mutual self-defence. Although they were constantly menaced by Jon Bull and his cohorts, the thistles also knew that when they were not under attack from them, they were at one and the same time being neglected in favour of the roses.

The thistles were then agreed as one: in order to survive as a group and to avoid both the neglect and the dangers posed by Jon Bull, they had to arrange for their seeds to be dispersed as far away as possible from him and his garden. It was common sense really, and the thistles knew it. All it needed was to persuade enough of their fellow thistles of the logicality of this position, and the thistle population would be safe and secure from the depredations of Jon Bull, his cohorts, his weed killers and his Wastemonister™ spade. Will a sufficient number of thistles take on board this simple and effective advice, and see for themselves the free and safe future that lies ahead of them, once their seeds start germinating in places beyond the power of Jon Bull and the control he currently holds over the flowers in his garden?

Watch this space ...

47 The "Freedom Jewel"

Jack Union was a thief. Of that, there was no doubt. In point of fact, he was what one might call a 'career criminal' and it was not unknown for him to prey on his neighbours as well as committing crimes further afield. Jack Union had turned one neighbour's – Dai's – water supply to his own house. He had also raided Dai's coal bunker so often that, by now, the latter had no coal left.

Jack Union's neighbour on the other side – Scott – had also suffered from Jack Union's depredations. Scott was an iron and steel merchant and very soon after he had moved in, Jack Union had seized any iron and steel that was lying about Scott's house and had sold it at a large profit for himself. This in turn funded Jack Union's gambling lust and as often or not he was to be found in the town casinos spending these profits, where he was accompanied by his bosom friend, Sam Washington. Only last night, the pair could have been seen in the Iraq Venture casino, dissipating their (often illegally obtained) money. Casino owners had become wise to Jack Union and Sam Washington's behaviour and had arranged things that they regularly lost money in their establishments. "No trickery in tricking a trickster" as the local saying went.

The police of course knew of Jack Union's behaviour but seemed either reluctant to act or maybe, and worse, they merely turned a blind eye to it. There were some who even alleged the police were bribed to stay quiet, and this would not have been that surprising, although it was as yet, not proven.

Naturally, with the local newspaper, the Daily Garbage, owned by Jack Union's friends, they were unlikely to rock the boat. Similarly, the local TV station, with its Director-General, BiBi See-Bias, in the pocket of Jack Union too, no adverse comment appeared in any media against Jack Union. It was often thought that a phone call or email from Jack Union to BiBi See-Bias was enough to ensure a favourable report of his activities and stop the revealing of any embarrassing details pertaining to Jack. Dai and Scott would rail furiously against this, but in reality, they had very little power in order to combat Jack Union's formidable influence in town.

Now, one could say the 'pinnacle' in Jack Union's 'career' as a criminal mastermind was the seizure of Scott's "Freedom Jewel" – a sparkling blue and white gemstone that Scott previously kept at home. The operation to take the jewel had taken place a few minutes after 5 p.m. – or to use the Continental fashion, 17:07, to be precise – one April afternoon.

Jack Union had then placed the "Freedom Jewel" in his safe and had kept it secure ever since.

Scott of course, was mad with rage at the theft and had been campaigning for the return of the blue and white "Freedom Jewel" since its theft. Knowing the police to be useless, he instead summoned his friends, Jacob Ite and Charlie Stewart to assist in recovering the gemstone. Sadly for Scott, both were soundly beaten by Redcotes, Jack Union's man-servant on the steps of Culloden House, where they met one April evening at just after a quarter to six, or 17:46, if you prefer. Charlie Stewart himself was lucky to escape for his life that day, as Redcotes whistled for his master's dog, Cumberland. Charlie Stewart fled, nursing a bloody nose.

But all does not appear lost. Word has reached Scott that a new attempt will be made shortly to enter Jack Union's house to recover the blue and white "Freedom Jewel," and force open the safe. An insider (believed to be the footman, Jenkins) has let it be known what the safe's combination code – 180914 – is. Scott is convinced that if he can rally enough friends together, then they can rush in on Jack Union, catch both himself and his cronies unawares and succeed in opening the safe.

The tantalising prize of recovering the blue and white "Freedom Jewel" will then be within their grasp – quite literally, in fact. It all depends on whether Scott has enough brave friends to accompany him in carrying out the task of returning the gemstone to its rightful owner. The preparations for the raid on Jack Union's house are going on apace and are getting very exciting.

We will soon see if Scott and his friends are successful in regaining the "Freedom Jewel."

48 Nobody's-Darling and McDoughnut

"I've been trying to write a parable to encourage a NO vote in the Scottish separation Referendum", Betray us Together Chief, Nobody's-Darling whined one day. "And I keep getting a mental block."

"You mean me, boss?" asked his faithful lieutenant, Bliar McDoughnut.

Nobody's-Darling ignored him.

McDoughnut tried again.

"What's the problem, boss?" he inquired.

"It seems to me," said Nobody's-Darling, "that the old adage 'the Devil has all the best tunes' is too true."

"How's that?" asked McDoughnut.

"Well," said Nobody's-Darling, "that Zion Rice Whatsit has written some forty seven parables for YES, and ..."

"I believe it's forty eight, now, boss" interrupted McDoughnut.

"Has written forty eight parables for YES," went on Nobody's-Darling. "He's a complete bloody amateur at telling stories and over 1 300 people on Facebook like his stuff. He's not even a bloody Scot, like you and me, McDoughnut!"

McDoughnut rolled his eyes, but said nothing. He didn't think it appropriate to remind his Chief, that he, Nobody's-Darling, had actually been born in England.

Nobody's-Darling was by now shouting in exasperation. "And another thing ..."

"Yes, boss?" said McDoughnut.

"And," resumed Nobody's-Darling, "we're the professionals when it comes to making up stories. And we bloody well can't come up with ONE to demonstrate the positive case for the Union."

"Hmmmmm." Bliar McDoughnut thought for a moment with his single brain cell – a Herculean effort for him. "You once had the idea of a horse and carriage, boss," he said brightly. "You know, 'they go together like love and marriage.' Like the Union between England and Scotland," he added helpfully.

"I did, McDoughnut." Nobody's-Darling sighed heavily. "And then I realised that those YES people could attack the image from so many different angles."

"How so, boss?" McDoughnut was very convincing as everybody's fool.

"Think about it, numbskull!" Nobody's-Darling's pursed his lips. "They'd say that a marriage often ends in divorce. That there was no love between Scotland and England at the time of their Union. That the horse was shackled to the carriage. That it did all the heavy, dirty, unpleasant work. That it was often whipped by its cruel and surly master in order to further that master's business. It was never out of its harness either." Nobody's-Darling let his head slump forward into his open palms.

McDoughnut nodded silently, a deep frown on his face.

There was a pause of about a minute. Then McDoughnut's face lit up.

"How about this then, boss?" he asked, his face wreathed in smiles. "Why don't we say the Union is like salt? It adds flavour to otherwise bland food!"

"No, McDoughnut, that will never work," replied Nobody's-Darling. He frowned and his eyebrows knitted at least two pullovers. "You see, McDoughnut, a lot of people are salt intolerant nowadays and so it wouldn't go down well with them."

"I see," said Bliar McDoughnut, his voice catching.

"Further," Nobody's-Darling went on, "Everyone agrees that too much salt is not good for the human body, in any case. The YES mob's medical people will quickly rubbish the story on that score, too."

"I see," repeated McDoughnut mechanically, his voice a barely audible whisper.

"Thirdly," Nobody's-Darling continued, ignoring McDoughnut, "to say that salt adds flavour to bland food is a definite non-starter. Don't you think those pesky YES supporters will state that we are thinking of Scotland as 'bland' and that it requires something to give it taste, something Union salt can? We can't go around insulting Scotland or talking it down.

We've already got, Iain 'Baldy Bruiser' Davidson and the BBC doing that, in any case. No, McDoughnut, that would never work."

"Sorry, boss," McDoughnut mumbled.

There was another awkward pause.

"We could say that Salmond and Sturgeon are power crazed fish," suggested McDoughnut, not very convincingly.

"Already been done," said Nobody's-Darling sharply. "Didn't work either – fish tend to work well together in schools and co-operate with each other. And education is a good thing: I remember Tony telling me once." Nobody's-Darling gave a wintery smile as he remembered easier, less-troubled times. "Education, education, education." He intoned wistfully.

"That's why we want to make it policy that all our students have to pay for it, if we win the Referendum, eh boss?" McDoughnut smirked.

"Not '*if*' ... but '*when*'" Nobody's-Darling returned his lieutenant's smile. "But," and the frown and furrowed eyebrows returned. "But, for now, McDoughnut, we have to combat this parable threat."

"I have a few other ideas, boss" said McDoughnut enthusiastically.

"Go on," replied Nobody's-Darling drily.

"Well," said McDoughnut, "how about 'the future's bright – the future's orange'? Some member of my Lodge suggested that one."

"Another organisation has used that one, you cretin!" Nobody's-Darling was shouting. "And don't you think all the YESsers would have a field day with that, and rub their hands with glee if we used that? We'd be forever associated with those

Neanderthals from Larkhall! Or apartheid-era leaders in South Africa!"

Bliar McDoughnut slumped in his chair opposite Nobody's-Darling in embarrassed silence.

"And don't think of a similar slogan, now that we've got an ex-Prime Minister offering his tuppence worth, too! 'The future's bright - the future's brown' has failure written all over it. On so many levels it's a clear no-no. People will associate it with that crummy Prime Minister – who incidentally hated my guts when I was his Chancer of the Exchequer – and a has-been politician. He never offered Scotland any more powers during his own Premiership, either." Nobody's-Darling's voice was reaching a crescendo. "And if we invoke the word 'brown', we are asking for trouble, McDoughnut!"

"How so, boss?" McDoughnut, who could be quite dense at times, asked as he squirmed in his chair.

"What colour are poopy-plops?" hissed Nobody's-Darling through gritted teeth.

"Oh!" McDoughnut looked crestfallen again, the colour draining from his cheeks.

There was another pause.

"I had thought of taking a leaf out of that Rice Williams's parables book and write a story about a train to More-Powers, arriving at its destination in 20:16," said Nobody's-Darling.

"Good one, boss!" cried a re-animated Bliar McDoughnut. "That's excellent!"

"But then I realised it would be too late arriving at its destination." Nobody's-Darling sighed a deep sigh. "And I hadn't banked on the train breaking down so often on its journey, either. It had started out at 17:07, but it didn't seem to be going anywhere, especially with all its engine problems and changes of driver. At this rate, it might not even arrive at New-Powers at 20:16."

Nobody's-Darling and McDoughnut sat facing each other over the desk in glum silence.

Finally, Nobody's-Darling spoke:

"That's it then, McDoughnut. Finished. *Kaput. Terminé.* We'll just have to concede that when it comes to describing the economy, quoting unemployment figures or estimating Scotland's oil wealth, we are masters at telling stories. But when it comes to presenting fun, interesting, informative and factual parables, then I'm afraid the NO Campaign has lost." He sighed. "We've lost."

Nobody's-Darling hung his head in his hands again.

"Let's hope we don't lose on 18 September, as well, eh boss?" McDoughnut said, "or we'll both be looking for new jobs."

Nobody's-Darling's head shot up like a startled pheasant and he gave McDoughnut a long withering look.

"Speak for yourself, Bliar McDoughnut," he said. "I already have my seat reserved in the House of Lords!"

49 Give us this day …

We cast our eyes over some highly-competitive bread products in our local supermarket, so that you will be able to make an informed choice about which one to buy. We will be awarding our own samples a grading of stars, up to a maximum of five – just like the Michelin Guides. Write in and tell us which one you will vote for.

The Editor, *Scottish Bakers Today* magazine.

1. <u>The Farage loaf</u>
First up is the Farage loaf. This loaf is a particularly white complexion. It contains no foreign ingredients and is made in part from the best UKIP flour. The

consistency of the texture makes it appear stodgy. Around the edges it may appear a little crusty, whilst the main part of the loaf is decidedly flaky. The taste is rather insipid, and we are tempted to say that the Farage loaf will not be to the taste of the majority of Scottish consumers. Being a purely white loaf of course means that not only is it bland in appearance but that it has no redeeming outside features which could add taste and flavour. If left out in the open, the Farage loaf tends to get mouldy and rotten very quickly, and in maintaining the traditional outlook in avoiding preservatives, it consequently will not keep for any long period of time.

Some of our tasters had to be led away with severe stomach cramps and vomiting after partaking of the Farage loaf. Treatment at nearby Neil's General Hospital was in order and upon recovery, our tasters have informed us that they will never touch a Farage loaf again. Those of you who still feel confident in acquiring one of these loaves should be aware that a Farage loaf is best suited to be stored rigidly vertical in the bread bin as this confers upon it the power and prestige it desperately craves, but in reality is only a self-publicist. If left out in the open for long periods of time, it has a tendency to become mouldy very quickly.

Scottish Bakers Today magazine opinion: 1 star (We're being generous)

2. The Westminster bun

Secondly, we present to you the Westminster bun. This is in effect half brown and half white. Its top is wholemeal, whilst its base is a standard white. The effort has been made to present the bun as "the best of both worlds" in that the wholemeal half and the white half complement and supplement each other.

However, the overall effect is one of a complete lack of harmony: the two colours clash with each other on immediate perusal. The bread roll is in fact neither fish nor fowl - half-baked, one is tempted to say. The wholemeal half may be pleasing to one faction and the white half enjoyed by another, but in essence, the composite does not work.

And it's not just the aesthetic qualities of this hybrid bread bun that jar; the taste does not succeed either. For devotees of white bread, the wholemeal additional flavour takes away from the natural enjoyment they would have had from a bun that was wholly white. In the same way, those who were persuaded that wholemeal bread was better or more enjoyable now have to suffer the indignity of sharing their favourite taste with the 'opposing' white flavour. Thus, the sum of its parts does not make for a harmonious whole.

Again, therefore, we suggest to the populace of Scotland that this should not be their bread of choice.

Scottish Bakers Today magazine opinion: 2 stars

3. <u>The Sturgeon loaf</u>

Our final selection was the Sturgeon loaf. This loaf immediately has great merit in that all its ingredients have be sourced from Scotland. They are thus of the highest quality and commend themselves to us as natural supporters of Scottish bakers. Being the in-house journal of the profession, we at *Scottish Bakers Today* have no compunction in saying that this is the bread of choice for Scottish households. It has a crisp yet firm texture and can be enjoyed either on its own or as a complement to such items as Essennpee cheese or in the making of sandwiches. Indeed, its versatility is probably unique in that the Sturgeon loaf will find its place in many recipe books, supplementing home Scottish cooking at its best. What better way to mop up your whisky sauce after an enjoyable haggis and a successful Burns Night that with a wedge of best Sturgeon bread?

Unlike most breads, the Sturgeon loaf will not crumble under pressure and can be enjoyed by all the family.

A winner in so many ways, we cannot praise this bread highly enough. As the saying goes, what you see is what you get with the Sturgeon loaf, and, if we may be so bold as to suggest, you will need no other bread for your family once you have chosen it. It will truly be your 'staff of life', your guiding principle and almost become part of your own family.

Scottish Bakers Today magazine opinion: 5 stars

50 They're all balloons!

Once upon a time, there were three balloons who were trying to establish themselves as the spokesballoon of their fellow red balloons. I say, 'red balloons,' but the reality of the situation rather proves otherwise. You see, upon closer examination, you would have discovered that there was a tinge of blue about all these seemingly 'red' balloons. It was rumoured that the shopkeeper no longer kept any purely red balloons in stock – they just didn't sell. In consequence our particular shopkeeper did not stock any other type of balloon, other than these reddish-blue balloons.

Now although these three balloons were essentially

of the same colour, they did have slight differences between them – differences which each one tried to market for himself/herself as standing apart from his/her compatriots.

The first reddish-blue balloon when inflated considered himself to be the most important balloon in the shop. This Murphy balloon had been especially imported from the central (southern) branch of the shopkeeper's store, and as a result tended to look down on what he considered the more 'parochial' balloons in the shop. He was not averse either to lording it over the other balloons and presenting himself as the 'must buy' balloon for the shop's customers. He also considered that the hot air with which he was carried was of a superior, Westminster brand, and so he had to be, almost by definition, the 'natural' spokesballoon on behalf of the other reddish-blue balloons.

The Murphy balloon had not, as yet however, settled into his position at the shop. Some of the other reddish-blue balloons were discomfited to learn that the Murphy balloon was (in their opinion) taking over their patch, claiming more hot air than he was entitled to and with the approval of the Chief Executive Officer of the shop chain (whose Head Office was based somewhere in the south) was sidelining the other reddish-blue balloons – those who had been in the shop much longer than he had.

These 'old guard' reddish-blue balloons were thus reminded of a similar situation where the Chief Executive Officer of the shop chain had imported in the Michael balloon (a similarly reddish-blue balloon) to the western branch of the shop some years previously. His presence there had similarly irked the 'local' balloons, (you could say his presence went down like a lead balloon), and so, in a show of unanimity, the reddish-blue balloons at the western branch shop had resolved to puncture the Michael balloon. This they duly did, resulting in a slow and painful deflation of the Michael balloon and the subsequent appointment of the Morgan balloon (a rather redder creature) in his place.

But we are being rather unfair here concentrating solely on the Murphy balloon and not referring to the other reddish-blue balloons in the shop, who were also in contention to be spokesballoon.

A seemingly quieter, Boyack balloon, had also presented itself as the representative of the rest of the balloons. However, being of a quieter disposition than any of the others, no one knew very much about her. She was, it was said, a worthy enough balloon, having been inflated on natural, green and environmentally friendly gases. But, and as so many of the reddish-blue balloons were, she was also noted to be full of hot air. Interest in the Boyack balloon outside the shop was negligible; indeed even within the group of reddish-blue balloons, she was something of a mystery. It was considered by some (rather cruelly, I feel) that she was not really capable of being inflated in any case, and that it would have been better had she been left in a dark corner, all wrinkled and unloved. It would come as no surprise if the Boyack balloon was not appointed the role of spokesballoon for the reddish-blue balloon tribe.

A third reddish-blue balloon also fancied his chances as being the leading representative of the clan of balloons in the shop.

The Findlay balloon prided himself as being a fixture of the shop since it had opened; a 'local' balloon in comparison to the 'interloping Murphy balloon.' Consequently, he had high hopes for himself in this regard and that he would be able to prevent the Murphy balloon from taking over the role of spokesballoon, and that he was better, far better than the Murphy balloon. He couldn't actually say this of course – the reddish-blue balloons had to show some sort of solidarity amongst each other, even if they were vying with each other as the lead spokesballoon of their tribe. The Findlay balloon was also said to have the support of the UNISON and UNITE air pumps, and this was considered by many outsiders to be a useful prop for the Findlay balloon to lean on, in order to be filled with its own version of hot air.

All in all then, the battle to become leading spokesballoon for the reddish-blue balloons looks set fair to be a bitter contest among the three mentioned above.

We'll just have to wait and see who has the most hot air!

51 Dear Catriona II ...

We're pleased to announce the return to your magazine of choice, *New Scotswoman Today*, the experienced and esteemed journalist, Catriona Alba who has decided to write for us in the capacity of agony aunt. She has a long and proud history of resolving disputes and of empathising with her readers. We invite you therefore, ladies and gentlemen (no sexism here at *New Scotswoman Today*), to write in with any problems you have and Catriona will answer them, for you. Here's the first letter Catriona has received.

The Editor, *New Scotswoman Today* magazine

Dear Catriona,

I am the new owner of the corner shop on Caledonia Street, Scotlandshire. The previous owner (known locally as Old Ma Lamont), decided to give up the premises recently. I heard that she wasn't given much say in what to stock on the premises, and that her landlady, Milly Band, was forever poking her nose into the shop's affairs.

Now, I am in charge of the corner shop on Caledonia Street. However, I have noticed that over the last few weeks, fewer and fewer customers are coming into the shop. What customers that are coming are buying less of my wares. I have tried offering them free bottles of Irn-Bru with every purchase, but even this does not appear to appeal to them. I have however noticed an increase in my egg and snake oil sales. I believe this to be a good sign.

I have even tried to hire a young and enthusiastic shop assistant – Kezza – behind the counter. But it looks to me that she doesn't appeal much to the residents of Caledonia Street, either. I accept that she's not the sharpest knife in the box – but you have to give youth their head, don't you?

Of course, I am not the only shopkeeper on Caledonia Street. I face strong competition from Sturgeon's Stores, a little way up the road. Now, and I am loath to admit it, Sturgeon's Stores is booming and their stock is flying off their shelves. Further, I could swear that more and more customers are getting their daily essentials from Sturgeon's Stores and not from my shop.

I took on board my current shop with the promise of turning it around and making it profitable. I also pledged to the good people of Caledonia Street that I would no longer be in thrall to my landlady, Milly Band, and she would let me run the shop in my own way.

It now appears to be the case, (and I am reluctant to admit it publically), that my shop is losing customers and income – it is in fact making great losses on most of its product lines.

Of course, I am averse in telling Milly Band all this – I do not want to lose face, especially after telling all the inhabitants of Caledonia Street that I was going to run the shop in my own way. Nor do I want to admit to my landlady and boss that I have been such a failure in turning round the fortunes of the shop on Caledonia Street.

Dear wee, Catriona – Whit shall I dae?

Yours in despair,

Jim M.
East Renfrewshire

52 Soup of the day?

We at *Scottish Grocers Today* magazine have been testing soups for you, our customers. We have awarded the different soups a star rating, up to a maximum of five – just like the Michelin Guides. Write in or tell us which one you think is the best soup and if you agree with our tasters' verdicts.

The Editor, *Scottish Grocers Today* magazine.

1   <u>Sturgeon broth</u>

A meaty and hearty soup, the Sturgeon broth warms and comforts the whole body. It is nourishing soul food and is therefore welcome all over Scotland –

especially when the climate is cold and harsh. Full of good, nourishing taste, it is a broth proven to keep undesirable Labconlib bugs at bay. Having no artificial additives or preservatives, the Sturgeon broth is guaranteed 100% Scottish. All in all, a very satisfying liquid, it comes highly recommended.

(5 stars)

2 Murphy soup

The Murphy soup is one which leaves a bad aftertaste in the mouth. As it is often served very hot, its heat and fieriness causing distress and harm to those who drink it. An attempt to add egg to the ingredients of the Murphy soup has backfired spectacularly on its manufacturers. The current texture will remind you of elements of Irn-Bru, with additional hints of snake oil. We strongly suggest that the Murphy soup is one best avoided.

(0 stars)

3 Dugdale soup

A thin, watery, weak and still rather youthful mixture. Decidedly, the Dugdale soup is not to everyone's taste; indeed many of our tasters found it to be insipid. A soup which is served lukewarm.

(2 stars – We're feeling generous on account of the youthfulness of this soup.)

4   Darling chowder

A cold liquid. The Darling chowder has rather a bland taste. Whereas (as previously noted) the Sturgeon broth can be considered to be an authentic 100% Scotch food, the Darling chowder can only aspire to anything approaching this, manufactured as it is in London. It only makes the grade in our survey here of Scottish soups due to its distinctive tartan packaging (© Messrs Kyle Yard (Productions) Ltd.). It has been suggested that the addition of some Union Salt® would improve the taste of this rather insipid chowder. However, we consider that not even this can save it from its uniform blandness. A chowder therefore we suggest which is unpalatable to most soup lovers. Not recommended.

(0 stars)

5   Baillie pottage

A full-bodied pottage, manufactured in Dumbarton and containing a lot of stock. The Baillie pottage will appeal only to those who appreciate a more mature type of soup. Keep away from children.

(1 star)

6   Curran soup

The Curran soup has pretensions of being a classic soup. In reality, it is however, a rather bitter soup to the taste – a flavour which it transmits readily to other foodstuffs which have either been already consumed or those eaten with it. A previously unknown chemical reaction when the Curran soup is served with Lamont croutons was observed by our tasters, which rendered the whole highly toxic. It is strongly suggested therefore that should any of our consumers wish to partake of the Curran soup, they do so avoiding Lamont croutons – and even then at their own risk. Previous experience had informed us that the Curran soup and Lamont croutons complemented and supplemented each other – but subsequent trials and tastings have demonstrated that this research was erroneous. That being the case, we strongly advise our consumers not to sample the Curran soup.

(0 stars)

And that completes our survey of the soups, chowders and pottages currently on the market. We will let you decide which one to choose, and which one you consider will have the best effect on you and your family for the foreseeable future.

53 Passenger announcement for those travelling by Free Caledonia Rail

"Good morning, ladies and gentlemen. Welcome aboard this Free Caledonia Rail express service to Independence, which is the end of the line and where this service will terminate. My name is Nicola and I am your chief guard on this train today. We started out from Essennpee at 19:34 and we will be calling at the following stations: Ewing Central, Devolution Halt, Parliament, Referendum Junction, Fortyfive Central, Newvote and Independence. Please note that owing to outside engineering work on the line, this could slightly delay our journey to our final destination. Additionally, work in replacing the track by outside contractors in the Devolution Halt area will mean that we will be shunted off the main track and find ourselves in the sidings for some time. However, please bear with us, as we hope to be back on the main track before too long and making up for that lost time. The train will pick up speed again after leaving Fortyfive Central. We wish you a pleasant onward journey with us and we thank you for travelling with Free Caledonia Rail."

54 An eminent psychologist writes …

Dear Scottish patients,

Many of you have been visiting my consulting rooms recently suffering from high blood pressure and a desire to hit out against various politicians wearing red, blue, yellow and purple rosettes when you have seen their pictures or when they have been having interviews on the television. Many of you also fear that as the General Election approaches, you will be suffering even more from this condition.

Let me reassure you all.

This condition, known to us in the medical profession as Unionitis (of which one particular strain is called *Smackus Murphyus*) is actually a common 'affliction' from which many people in Scotland are currently 'suffering.' I say 'suffering' in inverted commas, as I can tell you that this condition is not only very common in Scotland, but it is also completely benign. If you recognise the symptoms of high blood pressure, an increase in your sweariness, sweaty palms and a desire to throw a brick at the television should you see or hear David Cameron on the box, I can inform you that you are not alone in this 'affliction.'

Not being a malign condition, I cannot really see myself clear in saying that, as a layperson may have it, 'something is the matter with you.' You are a rational, reasonable citizen of Scottish society and should feel no shame to be 'suffering' from Unionitis. The form *Smackus Murphyus* has also resulted in an increase in the purchase of eggs – something which I'm sure you agree, is beneficial to the Scottish economy.

If however your concerns persist that you are indeed 'suffering' from something unpleasant, I hereby prescribe one 25mg Essenpee tablet (the yellow and black formula) to be taken after every meal.

May I wish you all the very best?

I must close this letter now as I have my next patient to see. Mr Milliband has serious delusions that he will be the next Prime Minister. I am sure that you will agree with me when I say his case is a very serious one.

Yours medically,

Sigmund Fried MSc, ABC, BBC, STV
Psychologist par excellence.

55 Hurricane Nicola

Once upon a time, a man called Jack Union decided to build a house. He collected together some blue bricks and started to lay the foundations to his house. But he was not happy with just blue bricks, so he found some red bricks and mortared them alongside the blue bricks. And then he found some yellow bricks and placed them in the west wall of his house.

He thought his house was then complete, until he realised that there was nothing upstairs. So he hurriedly found some purple bricks and put them to form an attic – he did not want people to think he had nothing upstairs.

Jack's house was now built and he stood back to admire his handiwork. He was very happy with his efforts. He called his new home, 'Westminster House' and he was very pleased with all that he had achieved in its construction. He could now spend the rest of his life in quiet contentment and he smiled as he thought of himself as lord of all that he surveyed. Nobody and nothing was going to mar his enjoyment of Westminster House. Or so he thought …

***

One evening, Jack Union was watching the news on his television in the plush living room of Westminster House. After the usual banalities involving celebrities and their latest tattoos and something about a green-minded Royal jetting off to some ecological conference where he could pontificate on the need to save the planet, the programme changed to the weather forecast.

Now, normally, Jack Union would not have given any credence to such a programme. Meteorologists were as accurate as Mystic Meg in predicting Lotto winners or those shysters who read your future from your palm at £5 a throw at village fêtes in Jack's opinion. According to Jack, fortune telling, and predicting the future, and that included stating what next Tuesday's weather was going to be like, was a load of crystal balls. And yet ... And yet, the sincerity with which the weather forecaster spoke unnerved Jack that night.

You see, the forecaster was convinced (and she said she had the support of many of her professional colleagues in the matter) that a large storm was brewing in the north of the country. She and her colleagues had already named the storm 'Hurricane Nicola', and it was growing in strength on a daily basis. On current estimates, Hurricane Nicola would wreak extreme damage on many properties currently owned by the large real estate company, Murphy Holdings plc, located in the north of the country.

The consensus (and the weather forecaster had to stifle a giggle at her own witticism at this point) was that Murphy Holdings plc would not be 'holding much property' after the passage of Hurricane Nicola.

Now, if that was not scary enough to Jack Union (he held a substantial amount of shares in Murphy Holdings plc), he then followed the presenter's right arm as it swept over the country. With a beating heart, short, irregular breaths and a lump in his throat, he saw that Hurricane Nicola's trajectory would sweep over the whole country. Westminster House and the surrounding village were in its direct path – in the eye of the storm, as it were. Jack Union swallowed thickly.

He was aware that there had been a few rumbling thunderstorms around Westminster House since his taking up residence, but he had taken very little notice of these. The most recent one, in September 2014, had initially threatened to demolish his property. As it turned out however, very little structural damage had occurred. Jack had got the builders to paint over the cracks with some red, white and blue paint. He also convinced himself that that was the end of the matter, and he could carry on living at Westminster House as he had previously. The painters involved, Smith, Lord and Kelvin Ltd., had done a thorough whitewashing job and Jack Union was pleased with their efforts.

Now it seemed their work was in vain. The meteorologists were convinced that Hurricane Nicola was on its (maybe 'her') and Jack Union's way. Nothing would be able to stop her progress. They advised Jack and others in the path of Hurricane Nicola to leave their residences (including Westminster House) that were the most likely to suffer a battering, as they feared that when (*not* 'if') the storm arrived, it was exceedingly likely that Westminster House would be completely destroyed and that Jack would be found under its rubble; at best severely bruised.

Jack was in a quandary. He did not want to believe the meteorologists or any other weather experts. Normally, he would have dismissed such talk of the destruction of Westminster House as, "scaremongering piffle." And he did not want to leave Westminster House. Yet he was fearful that if all the prognostics were correct, he would indeed become a casualty in his own home when Hurricane Nicola came and Westminster House collapsed around his ears.

With sweating palms, a pallid look on his face and swallowing heavily, Jack Union hauled himself up to bed. He would not have a restful sleep from now on until the arrival of the storm. The build up to Hurricane Nicola's appearance in his neck of the woods was proving to be very worrying to Jack Union, and there was nothing he could do about it.

56 Carmichael's the Butcher's

Carmichael's was a large butcher's shop, located at the far end of Orkney Street. It was very well known in town, but few people had actually seen the owner, known locally as 'Big Al,' if you'll excuse the pun, 'in the flesh.'

One day, a young lady, who was up on her holiday in the area from down south came into the butcher's shop. Her name was Tori Graff and she was looking for something to cook to go alongside her leek bake. She was holding a dinner party that very night and she wanted to impress her friends.

"How about some mince?" suggested the friendly shop assistant. "I find that leaks and mince complement each other very nicely."

Tori Graff was immediately impressed by the good-looking mince under the counter that she bought some there and then and took it home to cook.

But alas and woe! Having cooked it in the appropriate manner, (the leek bake however was not done so well and some would later whisper it was only half-baked), Tori Graff and her guests began to feel decidedly unwell. Could there be something the matter with Carmichael's mince?

The nearest Trading Standards Office was in the nearby town of Essennpee, and one of its officers was quickly called in. He promptly paid a visit to Carmichael's butcher's shop. The same assistant who had served Ms Graff the previous day was behind the counter – but he did not satisfy the man from Trading Standards: he wanted to see the Manager, 'Big Al' Carmichael himself.

After a long wait, 'Big Al' Carmichael shambled into the shop from the back. His nickname was well-earned: he was quite a large man, not out of place as a doorman at a nightclub, perhaps. Carmichael was wearing his standard butcher's apron and straw hat. He stared indignantly at the man from Essennpee Trading Standards.

"What's this all about, then?" he asked gruffly.

"We suspect that there is some issue with your mince," replied the Trading Standards Officer grimly.

"Poppycock!" exclaimed Carmichael. "I only sell the best quality mince in my shop. My meat is the best in town – you ask Mrs Cameron in Number 10. How dare you slander me like this!"

"Be that as it may," rejoined the Trading Standards Officer evenly, "I will still need to take a sample of your mince to study it in the lab. A rather virulent strain of *Libus Demus Smearus* is currently doing the rounds and I'ld like to do my duty to ensure – as you claim – that your meat products are not affected."

'Big Al' Carmichael harrumphed and swore blind that his mince was not contaminated. However, he could not very easily stop the Trading Standards Officer from Essennpee from upholding the law, so with a shrug of his shoulders, a deep groan and a defiant statement that he would be vindicated, 'Big Al' Carmichael shambled back to his office.

Essennpee Trading Standards were meticulous in their analysis of 'Big Al"s mince. All this cost a lot of money and a lot of time and effort was also expended, but when one considers that the safety and well-being of the town and possible breaches of the Food Act that were involved, Trading Standards did a thoroughly professional job.

The results from the laboratory eventually came through. As Essennpee Trading Standards had initially thought, there was a strong strain of the bacteria *Libus Demus Smearus* in 'Big Al' Carmichael's mince.

Upon hearing the result, the Trading Standards Officer acted promptly, and immediately returned to Carmichael's butcher's shop. Again, there was a lengthy delay before the man himself appeared, clad as usual in his butcher's apron and straw hat.

"I have to inform you that you have been found selling food which is unfit for human consumption," announced the Trading Standards Officer from Essennpee gravely. "To whit, your mince has been proven to contain a most unpleasant strain of *Libus Demus Smearus*," he went on. "This has been demonstrated to be the cause of the ill-effects in everyone who has swallowed your mince."

'Big Al' Carmichael was silent for a little while.

Then he blurted out,

"It wasnae me! It was my shop assistant … It was Mundell! He made me do it!"

"Be that as it may," replied the Trading Standards Officer. "This is a strict liability offence under the Food Act." He paused for his words to sink in. "I will be obliged to make a report that Carmichael's the Butcher's should be closed forthwith and that you will never sell any meat product ever again in the future."

"B-b-b-b-ut you can't do that!" stuttered 'Big Al' Carmichael. "Think of my livelihood. My good name here on Orkney Street." He paused. "I am NOT going to submit to your blackmailing innuendo, sir!" 'Big Al' was shouting.

"We shall see what Mr Justice Scott and Mrs Justice Shetland have to say when we take you to court, Mr Carmichael," replied the Essennpee Trading Standards Officer with a smile as he walked out of the shop, into the sunshine.

Will 'Big Al' Carmichael now face the chop?

Watch this space ...

The Author

Siôn Rees Williams was born in Llanelwy/St. Asaph, Cymru/Wales in 1968 and was subsequently brought up and educated in Welsh, English, French and Latin in West Sussex, Gwynedd and West Yorkshire. He holds an MA Degree in Celtic Studies out of the University of Wales Trinity Saint David and an LLB. (Hons.) Degree in Business Law from the University of Huddersfield. Siôn defines himself as "a lawyer by training, a linguist by profession and a nationalist by conviction."

He is also a qualified and experienced teacher of Welsh (his first language), English and French to adults and students. Latterly, he was the sole Associate Lecturer in Welsh for the Open University, East of England region. Prior to that he taught the language at John Paul II Catholic University of Lublin, Poland for two years and on a freelance basis, through the medium of French in Paris, France for almost five years. He has represented, as sole exhibitor/language teacher, both Wales and Welsh at two international language fairs – Expolangues, Paris, 1998-2000 and annually since 2006 and Expolingua, Praha/Prague, Czech Republic, 2007-2009.

A competent and accomplished trilingual translator and editor in Welsh, English and French, Siôn has worked for many companies and organisations in order for their message to be conveyed effectively and presented accurately to the general public. Past clients have included Census 2011, Editions Hachette, Her Majesty's Government, LOCOG, Michelin, Pfizer Inc., Principality Building Society, Royal Mail Ltd., TV Licensing Ltd. and Vodafone.

Although Siôn is an active member of both Plaid Cymru and the SNP, as well as many Welsh pressure groups – and many of the parables here echo his core political beliefs in regard to the nations these parties represent – he has a lifelong empathy with minority peoples from all over the globe. He therefore firmly believes that these parables will find echoes in other places where smaller cultures are threatened by others and where the trend towards uniformity of thought and action seems to be all-prevalent. The parables therefore should not be taken as being against any particular individual, ethnic group or nation. There is nothing incompatible in wanting the best, and freedom for one's own country and respecting others' rights to the same and even acknowledging – if not agreeing with – those who hold an opposing point of view.

Siôn Rees Williams lives with his wife, Miranda and their cat, Viola, in Bedfordshire, England.

More information on the author can be found on his web site:

http://uk.linkedin.com/in/sionrwilliams

Printed in Poland
by Amazon Fulfillment
Poland Sp. z o.o., Wrocław